The Beginner's Book of
Bread Making

The Beginner's Book of
Bread Making

Diana Dasey

with photographs and illustrations by Josh Dasey

This book contains more than 65 tested recipes for yeast breads —
from basic breads to celebration, ethnic, healthy, fun breads and sourdoughs,
to sweet and trendy breads, rolls and buns.

Kangaroo Press

Dasey, Diana
The Beginner's Book of Breadmaking.
Includes index.
ISBN 0 86417 767 4
I. Bread. I. Title
641.815

Illustrations and photography: Josh Dasey

First published in 1996 by Kangaroo Press Ltd
3 Whitehall Road Kenthurst NSW 2156 Australia
PO Box 6125, Dural Delivery Centre NSW 2158
Printed in Hong Kong by South China Printing Co. (1988) Ltd

Contents

Introduction

This book is for anyone who has ever wanted to make bread but thought it was far too hard. It's for those of you who may have unpleasant memories of the only time you've tried to make bread, ended up with hard rocks instead, then vowed never to attempt it again. It is also for those of you who think you must have a long family tradition of bread making if you want to bake a loaf of bread.

I remember my first experience of bread making and the first time I met and used yeast.

I was twelve and it must have been before Easter as the cooking class I was in was making hot cross buns. Cooking classes at my school, in a small Queensland country town, were never happy times and it took many years before I realised that cooking could be joyous and delightful and creative and fun and many happy and interesting hours could be spent playing in kitchens.

In that classroom kitchen we rarely cooked the foods that most children love — the fried goodies, the biscuit treats and the sweet things. Instead we prepared the dishes the education authorities of the time thought necessary for our future lives as wives and mothers. I think they may have supposed our husbands and children were going to be a very sickly lot as there was a heavy emphasis on foods for convalescents and invalids. We cooked food without colour and with not much taste. We steamed nearly everything — eggs, custards, puddings, vegetables, meats. We made odd dishes like raw beef tea with scraped beef in a tumbler of cold water seasoned with salt and pepper and swallowed in one gulp — if you could. We used shredded beef suet to make the suet crust for roly poly jam puddings and we tied flannel to the upturned legs of a chair to strain the apples and juice to make apple jelly.

Our teacher was a cranky old woman who scolded and nagged us all the time and made us feel that enjoying eating wasn't quite nice or refined. We learned not to listen to anything she said and, when we realised that the cooking classes were not to be fun or the good eating feasts we thought they may have been, the one thing we all looked forward to was the surreptitious sampling of all the food stores in the kitchen cupboards. Grubby little-girl fingers secretly dipped themselves into the desiccated coconut, the dried fruit, the powdered milk and, if we were very lucky, into the opened can of sweetened condensed milk in the refrigerator. We stuffed our sticky fingers into our greedy mouths and, if it was good eating, we went back again for more.

I didn't go back for a second taste of fresh yeast. It made my mouth pucker and I didn't like it one little bit — I didn't like the buns that I made either. The crosses on the tops were lopsided and wrong and the buns, not at all like the ones from the local cake shop, were small and hard and horrible. I remember how disappointed I was.

At home there was no family tradition of bread making. My mother, even though she was Queensland country born and a really good cook, didn't bake bread at all and spoke with great respect of women who did.

I started serious bread making when I was in my twenties and, once again, it was hot cross buns. I still remember the buzz I had at the praise my second pitiful effort won me. We ate them very hot, just out of the oven minus the crosses (they were too hard), with lots of butter and jam and they were a great success even though I knew they were only marginally better than the ones I made at school.

I went on to make other yeast breads, mostly eaten very hot with lots of butter and jam, and was regarded as something of a wonder woman by my husband and our friends. I was never quite sure of what I was doing and the bread books I started buying were either incredibly vague about quantities, presumed greater skills and knowledge than I had or listed ingredients I'd never heard of. Somehow the breads I made became better and better and we ate them, even after they'd cooled, and with a little less butter and jam. When I was asked to write a book on bread making several years ago I was rather startled but, as my life has been based on a frivolous 'why not?' philosophy rather than anything more profound, I signed the contract, spent the advance money and then wondered what sort of book to write. I haunted libraries, spoke to friends and cooks, looked at all the cookbooks I had and bought lots more. As before, I was intimidated by some and irritated by others and decided the only way for me to go was to write the sort of book on bread I'd like to have found when I first started bread making. And so I did. But that first book of mine on bread making owed a lot to the thoughts and opinions of other people — so unsure I was of my bread making and myself. Some of the recipes I really liked but many were ones I thought other people would expect to find and it didn't matter whether I really cared for them or not.

As I changed over the years, and learnt to worry less about the opinions and views of others, my bread making changed. Now I rarely follow anyone's recipe when I make bread and I do it as easily as I make a good cup of coffee. Of course, I know what I am doing. I've learnt from my early disasters that there are some rules you just can't ignore. It really is vital not to kill the yeast with too much heat, bread making flour is a very great help, kneading for long enough is really necessary and letting the dough rise at least once before baking is not just a good idea, it's essential.

These days the sorts of bread I bake vary and always depend on the way I am feeling at the time. Sometimes I bake trendy breads, sometimes ethnic, often fun and foolish, occasionally weird and wonderful but hardly ever very serious breads.

This book only has recipes in it that I like. This book is for me. I hope you like it too.

Diana Dasey

Ingredients

Flour

The one flour that should always be included in all bread recipes (if you want a light well-risen loaf) is wheat flour. The wheat flour contains a high percentage of the protein gluten, a vital ingredient in the successful bread making process.

When wheat flour is mixed with liquid, stirred, beaten and kneaded, the gluten in the flour changes and forms a rubber-like substance. This rubbery stuff stretches like elastic to hold the gases that escape from the growing yeast, and so the bread rises. Some flours have a low percentage of gluten and others just don't have any at all. So, if you want a light, high loaf, it is very necessary to have some wheat flour, either plain or wholemeal (whole-wheat), in whatever bread you make. If you really want a very dense, heavy bread, you can forget about using wheat flour altogether.

Even with wheat flour, you need to find the flour with the highest percentage of gluten as some wheat flours have a low gluten content. Professional cooks call low gluten flours 'soft' and use them for cakes and pastries. Bakers choose a flour with a high gluten content, called 'strong', and use that for their bread.

Finding flour with a high gluten content is simple if you want to buy a large quantity, as most flour mills will happily sell you a 25 kg (50 lb) pack. For smaller quantities you can find bread making flour in health food stores and very occasionally in supermarkets. But buying any packet of plain (all-purpose) flour is a chancy business as some flours will be soft and the finished bread will be disappointing. If you've made bread with a cake-like texture, you had the wrong sort of flour.

One way of increasing the gluten content in your flour is to sift one level teaspoon of gluten flour with every cup of other flour that you are using. This is the only time that I do any sifting in bread making, but if you don't thoroughly blend the gluten flour with the other flour, the gluten flour will form nasty little lumps throughout your bread.

You can tell if flour is good for bread making by its feel. Cake flour feels very soft if you plunge your hand into it, while flour for bread making feels almost gritty. I sometimes buy flour from my local supermarket and I've found that the plain flour in the most expensive packaging is usually soft cake flour and the cheaper packaged flours are strong flours and good for bread making. I never buy supermarket generic branded flour as these flours are not consistent and can sometimes be right for bread and sometimes not. Other flours that you can use in bread making are rye, buckwheat, coconut, cornmeal (polenta), chick pea, lima bean, millet, oat, peanut, potato, rice, soy and water chestnut.

In time you'll become so casual and confident about bread making that you'll find yourself switching flours at will. You'll answer as vaguely as I do when asked what sort of flour I've used in a loaf: 'Oh, I don't know, really...a bit of this and a bit of that'. But I always add wheat flour and it's usually white.

In many bread recipes from overseas, unbleached flour is often suggested. The main reason for bleaching flour is to give it a uniform appearance that we, the consumers, expect and demand. Flour from the USA is milled from a variety of grains and can have a multicoloured look and so it is often chemically bleached white, a process that destroys some of its nutrients. Australian flour is more uniform in colour and doesn't need the same treatment and is usually not bleached. The difference between the two flours is obvious — unbleached flour is creamy; bleached flour is very white and looks like cornflour (cornstarch). Also refer to the glossary (page 131).

Yeast

Yeast is a living micro-organism. Like all living things, it does its best when treated properly. It needs moisture, air to breathe and food to grow on. It will grow in quite cold conditions, such as in the deep freezer, but only very slowly. While it is growing, yeast produces bubbles of carbon dioxide and alcohol. This gas enters the framework of the gluten in the dough and forces it to stretch and rise. For quick growth, gentle warmth is needed, but not too much. The top of the stove can often be far too hot. You can easily tell if you've placed your dough in too hot a place if the dough feels really warm. Don't ever let your doughs get too hot because, if you do, the yeast will die and your bread will never rise.

Yeast is available in two forms — fresh and dried. Both give good results so choose the one that suits your needs and nature. If you think ahead about your baking and can remember to buy fresh yeast from delicatessens and health food stores, use that. It does work faster than the dried. But if you are an 'I just feel like making bread and I don't care it's midnight and all the shops are shut' person then dried yeast is handy to have. Most makers of it now claim that it works as fast as fresh yeast, but I am not totally convinced about that. Sachets of dried yeast contain 7 g (¼ oz) and can be substituted for 20 g (¾ oz) of fresh yeast.

The amount of yeast to use in relation to the flour can vary from recipe to recipe. I use 20 g (¾ oz) of fresh yeast or one sachet of dried yeast to about four cups of flour in basic breads without much oil or fat, eggs, sugar or milk. In richer breads I use more. For speedier results you can increase the yeast but doughs that are slower to rise have more flavour and character than rapidly risen doughs. You can use half the quantity of yeast specified in most of the recipes in this book and your breads will have more flavour but will be slower to rise.

Liquids

When you first start your bread making it's probably easier to use water; lukewarm for fresh yeast and warm for dried yeast; but if you use milk, there is no need to scald or boil it, as often instructed in many bread recipes.

Those recipes were written in the days of unpasteurised milk and precautions were needed as raw milk has enzymes that can interfere with the growing yeast. Commercial bakers always use sterilised milk in their baking so their results are always the same but there's no need for you to do it. However, if you feel very unhappy about not scalding the milk, by all means, continue to do so.

Your choice of liquids depends on what taste and result you want. Water breads have a heavy crisp crust while milk gives a velvety grain and a soft crust. You can also play around with butter-milk, sour cream, yoghurt, skim milk, fruit juice, chicken stock, beef gravy, beer, coffee, tea, wine, soy milk, vegetable cooking water, rice water, soups and soft drinks.

The only thing that really matters is that liquids be at the right temperature to ensure the gentle fast growing of the yeast and not the rapid killing of it. You need around 37°C/98°F for fresh yeast and 43°C/110°F for dried yeast (which needs the extra heat to get it working).

No-one ever really needs a thermometer in the kitchen — I don't anyway — but I remember babies bottle temperatures and aim for that for lukewarm water. I get this by mixing one part of hot water with two parts of cold, but your hot water system may be hotter than mine. Mix the water and then test it with a finger or two. If it feels hot, it is too hot for fresh yeast. For dried yeast, I mix equal parts of hot and cold water.

Fats

You use fats in bread for flavouring, tenderness and to keep it fresh. You can use any sort of oil or shortening or fat you have but, as a guide, I usually use a light flavoured oil for breads and always butter or margarine for sweet doughs. You can add flavour as well with bacon fat, cooked chicken fat, or homemade beef dripping.

Sugars

Sugars are not totally necessary in bread making. True, French bread, for instance, does not have any, but sugars do add flavour and help feed the growing yeast. Simple white sugar is fine for most breads but try playing around with brown sugar, golden syrup, treacle, molasses, jam, marmalade or malt. Honey has a bonus as a sweetening agent as it helps keep bread moist, but use only pale coloured mild tasting honeys as dark ones can have too strong a taste and, as well, may interfere with the growing of the yeast.

Salt

You can always tell when you've forgotten to put the salt in your bread — it tastes flat. But salt does much more in bread making than just giving bread a better flavour. Salt also prevents the yeast from working too fast, it strengthens the gluten in the flour so the bread has a good structure and it keeps the bread moist. For those of you on a totally salt free diet, by all means use a salt substitute but be prepared for a loaf that is not completely successful.

Other ingredients for bread

EGGS

You add eggs to make richer breads with a golden colour. Have the eggs at room temperature or, if you forget to do this, stand them in a cup of lukewarm water to take the chill off them. As well as adding flavour, eggs act as an emulsifier and breads with eggs will last longer than breads without them. Lecithin granules have the same emulsifying effect as eggs. Use 2 level teaspoons of granules as a substitute for each egg.

HERBS AND SPICES

Any bread can be completely changed by herbs and spices. Until you are sure you like the taste, only add small amounts at first and be a little cautious with herb and spice combinations as some work very well and others just don't. Fresh herbs always have a better flavour than dried, but if you need to substitute dried ones use only one-third of the quantity.

NUTS

Use only the freshest of nuts and never buy ones for 'baking' as their bitter taste uncooked is worse when cooked. I coarsely chop nuts for my breads but if you want them whole or very finely ground, it won't matter at all.

SEEDS AND GRAINS

You can add any sort of seeds or grains to any loaf, either on top of the bread or inside it. Always cook grains before using as they don't cook in the bread while it bakes.

Working with yeast

Mixing by hand

Place the yeast in a large mixing bowl, add the water, lukewarm (about 37°C/98°F) for fresh yeast and warm (about 43°C/110°F) for dried yeast, and stir until the yeast softens and dissolves a little. Add the salt, the sugar, the oil (if you are using it) and half of the flour and beat very well with a strong wooden spoon.

Add almost all of the remaining flour, a half a cupful at a time. When the dough becomes too hard to work with the spoon, use just one floured hand to pull the dough together in the bowl. You don't have to use just the one hand but I've seen some people being very distressed in classes with two messy hands. Besides, it's always good to have one hand clean to answer the telephone if it rings.

Kneading by hand

Kneading often worries people in my classes but there is more than one way to do it. You simply keep the dough moving around the board in any manner you like and find easy. If you've worked with clay in pottery classes, use the same technique. The method I use is to fold the dough towards me with my fingers and then push it away with the heel or side of my hand. I give the dough a quarter turn and keep repeating the action. All that matters with kneading is pushing the dough around — it helps rid the body of any aggressions if you can do it in a smooth, soothing and rhythmical way.

Being comfortable as you knead is very important as working on a surface that is too high or too low can be unpleasant and harmful. To find out the right height for you, stand next to a bench or tabletop or work surface and bend your elbows to an angle slightly greater than 90°. If your hands touch (or very nearly touch) the top, that's a good height to knead on. The easiest kneading action starts from the shoulders so you use your whole arms and keep your back straight.

I like to knead on my kitchen benchtop, which is a little high for me but the laminated wooden top is so smooth and so good that the dough never clings to it. I don't like untreated wood boards for kneading but any laminated surface is fine and so are large white plastic chopping boards. If you think the dough is sticking too much, find a smoother surface. Some doughs will stick so use a knife to scrape off dough that does and if you must use water and a cloth be sure that you dry the surface thoroughly. I once had a smooth marble slab for pastry and it worked well for doughs except they rose more slowly because they were always very cold.

Kneading times will vary from person to person. It all depends on the muscles and enthusiasm of the kneader. As a rough guide, knead for a minimum of five minutes vigorously or ten minutes leisurely. Knead until the dough isn't sticking to your hands or the board and it is smooth and elastic. Use just a very light scattering of flour on the board (never on top of the dough) to stop the dough from sticking.

Don't skimp on the kneading as your bread will suffer. Dough that has been kneaded enough has a wrinkled, textured look and feels springy, elastic and resilient. Simple white doughs feel as soft as young tender skin and, if you think you have kneaded enough, there are two tests I've found that work well.

The first test is to press into the dough with your fingers and if the dents in the dough disappear quickly you've done enough kneading. The other one is to pinch off, with floured fingers, a ball of dough the size of a golf ball and gently stretch it as thinly as possible. Insufficiently kneaded dough tears very quickly but dough kneaded well will stretch like elastic.

The amount of flour you knead into your dough varies but, as a general rule, breads you plan to bake in a pan can be a little softer than free-form breads that you want to shape and bake on a baking tray on their own.

By mixer fitted with a dough hook

Place the yeast in a large mixing bowl, add the water, lukewarm (about 37°C/98°F) for fresh yeast and warm (about 43°C/110°F) for dried yeast, and stir until the yeast softens and dissolves a little. Add the salt, the sugar, the oil (if you are using it) and almost all of the flour and mix, using the dough hook and a low speed, until the dough comes together and leaves the sides and bottom of the bowl.

Knead for three minutes, adding the extra flour if necessary. Then, knead by hand on a lightly floured board for one minute or until the dough is no longer sticky.

By food processor

Place the yeast in the food processor bowl fitted with the steel blade. Add the water, lukewarm (about 37°C/98°F) for fresh yeast and warm (about 43°C/110°F) for dried yeast, and pulse until the yeast softens and dissolves a little. Add the salt, the sugar, the oil (if you are using it) and almost all of the flour and process, with several pulses to mix, for about one minute. Add enough of the remaining flour so that the dough comes together. Then, knead by hand on a lightly floured board for one minute or until the dough is no longer sticky.

If you have a small food processor, process the dough in two batches and do not overwork dough.

The first rising

Place about a tablespoon of any bland tasting oil in a large bowl. Place the dough into the bowl and turn the dough over so that it is very thinly coated all over with a little oil. You do this to prevent a hard skin forming on the dough and stopping a smooth even rising. Put the bowl in a large plastic bag (any colour is fine) to keep the moisture in and draughts out or, if you prefer, cover the top with plastic cling wrap.

Leave the bowl in a warm place until the dough grows and doubles in size. Warm spots in summer are easy to find but never put the dough out in the direct sun as, if it is a really hot summer's day, the dough can start cooking in the bowl. In winter use a warmed pottery or glass bowl.

Finding warm spots can be a creative challenge. Everyone loves the idea, and it really works, of using your bed and your electric blanket. Other warm spots can be a cold oven with a pan of hot water under it; in a cold oven with the light switched on; in a sink or bath with warm water around the bowl; near, but never on, a radiator; in a warmed-up, switched-off electric fry pan; on top of a working clothes dryer; or just look for any place your cats find warm and use that. If you put the dough in a place where the dough feels hot, then that place is too hot. Your bread may rise, if you haven't completely killed the yeast, but it will stale very quickly and will have a very yeasty taste.

It's difficult to give a completely accurate time on how long it will take for a dough to grow and double in size. It will depend on how much yeast is used, the warmth of the place where the dough is rising and what ingredients are used in the recipe. As a guide — a plain dough with 20 g (¾ oz) of fresh yeast or 1 sachet of dried yeast with only water, salt, a little sugar and about four cups of flour; in a warm and cosy environment of about 26°C/80°F; will take from 45 to 60 minutes to grow. If your dough hasn't moved at all in this time then you have killed the yeast and there is nothing you can do to resurrect it so be brave — throw it out and start again with liquid that is not too hot.

The punching down

Punching down or knocking down means just that. Make a fist and push down into the centre of the dough. There's no need to be really violent as the dough will collapse very easily. Pull the edges of the dough into the centre and knead lightly just to get rid of the air and to bring the dough back to its original size. If you overhandle the dough you may find it won't go into the shape you want it to. Cover it with a cloth and leave it alone for five minutes for it to relax and be more manageable.

The shaping

You can shape the dough any way you like. If you think it is very soft, consider baking it in a pan. Special baker's pans are wonderful to own but don't put off bread making until you save up enough money to buy them. Use what you have in the cupboard. Any round, square, rectangular, star, heart, cylinder or loaf pan is fine. Use a springform pan, a ring pan, a casserole dish, a fluted pan, a billy can, a seasoned terracotta pot or, if you really don't have or want any pans at all, use any sort of food can. Just use your imagination but do make sure the container is ovenproof and well greased. I like to use melted butter or margarine as I don't think oil works well.

FOR BREAD BAKED IN A PAN

Just drop the ball of dough into any greased pan or, if you want to make a loaf with a better texture, flatten the dough into an oval shape and roll it up. Pinch the ends together and place, with the smooth side uppermost, in a greased pan. The only rule for baking in a pan is to only fill half of the pan with the dough.

FOR FREE-FORM BREAD

Make sure the dough is firm enough to hold its shape on its own without the support of a pan. After you have punched it down and given it a short knead, let it rest on the board. It should be firm enough not to spread all over the place. It needs to give just a little relaxing sag, but if it goes all over the board work in a little more flour and then shape in whatever basic or fanciful way you like. You can play with your dough and make round, oval, long, curled, plaited, stacked or twisted loaves or form any wild and wonderful shape you can. Just aim for a loaf that has a smooth top and a tight surface tension. Place the shaped dough on a greased baking tray.

The second rising

This second rising will take about half the time of the first rising. Cover the dough with a light dry cloth and leave in the same warm place to rise until once again it has doubled its bulk. It's always easy to tell when doughs in pans are ready to bake. When the dough rises to the top of the pan it is time to put it into the preheated oven.

For free-form doughs use the same finger test as before (in the section *Kneading by hand,* page 15), but this time if the indentations remain, or fill slowly, the dough is ready for baking. If doughs overgrow upon this second rising then lose their shape and collapse, simply knead lightly, re-form and let them rise again.

The decorations

Before or after the dough has risen for the second time you can cut patterns and symbols in the top of the dough. You choose what look you want. If you want a really opened out pattern, cut or slash before rising. If you want a tighter look, cut or slash just before placing the bread into the oven. Use a very sharp thin knife, a new single edged razor blade, kitchen scissors or a sharp scalpel to make shallow cuts in the dough. You can do crisscrosses, notches, slashes, herringbones, scrolls, diamonds, an initial and so on.

The glazing and finishing touches

Glazes add a finishing touch to your breads before or after you bake them. They can be as simple as spraying with water so that the seeds or nuts you want to sprinkle on the top stay attached, or brushing with milk for a soft dark crust. An egg beaten with a little water or milk gives a rich brown glow as it bakes. I like to use the simplest of all finishes — a lavish sprinkling of flour all over the risen dough. Spreading butter over the top crust of a loaf just baked adds flavour and keeps the crust soft. Spraying with water as the bread cools makes a very crisp crust.

The baking

Preheat your oven for at least 15 minutes before baking your risen loaves. You'll know when the oven is ready when the oven light goes off for the second time. If you do not have an oven indicator light use an oven thermometer. Bake on the second bottom or middle shelf and always allow 5 cm (2 in) of space between the pans and the sides of the ovens. Don't overload the oven or use baking trays that are too big as they will prevent the heat from circulating. Usually plain simple doughs are baked at high temperatures of between 200°C (400°F) and 220°C (425°F) and rich doughs with eggs and butter are baked at 180°C (350°F).

Another guide is to bake breads, that you want soft on the inside, quickly in a moderately hot oven (200°C/400°F). If you want with a thick hard crust on your bread, bake them more slowly in a moderate oven (180°C/350°F). Bread isn't as temperamental as sponge cakes but don't open the oven door for the first ten minutes of cooking. Intense heat is needed during this time as the bread has its final growing time and the yeast is finally killed.

Cooking times are given as a guide only as every oven is different and has its own funny little ways. If you think your temperatures are not right, instead of buying a new stove, buy an oven thermometer. Place it on a centre shelf and test your oven heat and you may find you do not need a new stove after all.

Use the times given in the recipes as a guide only and use all of your own senses to tell when the bread has cooked enough. If it looks brown, it could be baked; if there is no stale beer smell and it smells wonderful, it's done; if it sounds hollow when you tap it on its well browned bottom your bread is fully cooked.

Most ovens bake unevenly and often have troublesome hot spots. I like to do all of my baking on a layer of unglazed terracotta quarry tiles that were rejects in a tile shop and were very kindly given to me for nothing. These diffuse the heat evenly and my breads and cakes rise and bake with more level tops. If I want a really crisp crust on my French breads, I place a pan of boiling water on the floor of the oven or toss in ice cubes to generate the steam needed for a crispy exterior.

The cooling and storing

Turn bread out of pans and slide the free-form loaves off their baking trays onto wire racks to cool so that the air can circulate around them completely. If you want the crust really crisp, place the bread in a draught. If you want a softer crust, cover with a cloth. Leave breads to cool for at least an hour before cutting, but if no one wants to wait as long as that use an electric knife for cutting or tear the bread rather than cutting with a bread knife. When the bread is completely cold, store in sealed plastic bags in the refrigerator or freezer.

Tools of the trade

For storage

- plastic garbage bins
- screw top glass jars

I use lined plastic garbage bins to store the large quantities of flour I use in classes. I fold the liners over the flour before securing the lids. I also add bay leaves as, I've been told, the little creatures that can live in flour don't like the smell of bay leaves and won't want to breed. For smaller quantities of flour, a short time in the deep freezer will kill any insects or eggs in the flour. I then store the flours in sealed glass jars. Flours with a high fat content, such as wheat germ and soy flour, need to be bought in small amounts and kept frozen or chilled.

For assembling

- plastic wash up bowls
- small mixing bowls

When I first started bread making I was convinced I couldn't make bread at all unless I had a heavy large English china mixing bowl with sloping sides so the dough could rise up those sides. The English bread books I read kept telling me I had to have them. The bowls were very expensive but I saved up and bought myself one. I loved it until somehow it was broken and I shouted at the child who had broken it.(And so was the replacement one and I was the culprit then.)

I found bowls from Asia which were just as heavy but cheaper and bought them when I started teaching bread making in community halls and had to take my own equipment. They were very hefty to carry and people kept breaking them (and I couldn't shout at them). I thought there had to be an easier and lighter way and decided that even though plastic bowls were totally untraditional, and really designed for washing, they would do just as well. And, even though the sides don't slope, the dough still manages to rise beautifully.

Mixing and measuring

- strong wooden spoons
- measuring cups and spoons
- rubber scrapers
- rolling pin
- pastry brushes
- a large smooth surface for kneading
- plastic bags

I've used metric measuring cups and spoons in these recipes because that is what I have but **you can use whatever cup measure you like. Just be sure you use the same cup measure for everything** — the flour, the water, the other liquids — otherwise you may end up with dough which is too stiff and is very difficult, if not impossible, to put right. A dough which is too soft is easy — it just needs more flour.

OPTIONAL

- an electric mixer with a dough hook
- a food processor

For baking

- Special baker's pans or any ovenproof container of any kind such as any round, square, rectangular, star, heart or cylindrical loaf pan; a springform or fluted pan; a ring tin; a casserole dish; a billy can; a seasoned terracotta pot prepared by soaking in boiling water, drying and brushing lavishly with lots of butter; any sort of food can for fruit juice, tomato paste, dog food or baked beans.

The Breads

Simple Plain White Bread

20 g (¾ oz) fresh yeast or
  1 sachet dried yeast
1¼ cups water, lukewarm
  for fresh yeast, warm for
  dried yeast
2 level teaspoons salt
2 level teaspoons sugar
1 tablespoon oil or melted
  butter or melted lard
3½ to 4 cups bread
  making flour or 3½ to
  4 cups plain (all purpose)
  flour sifted with 3 level
  teaspoons gluten flour

GLAZE
water or milk

BY HAND
PLACE THE YEAST in a large mixing bowl, add the water and stir until the yeast softens and dissolves a little. Add the salt, sugar, oil and half of the flour and beat very well with a strong wooden spoon. Add almost all of the remaining flour, a half a cupful at a time. When the dough becomes too hard to work with the spoon, use just one floured hand to knead the dough in the bowl.

TURN ONTO a lightly floured board and knead for five minutes or until the dough no longer sticks to your hands or the board and it is smooth and elastic. Use just a very light sprinkling of flour on the board to stop the dough from sticking.

BY MIXER
PLACE THE YEAST and water in a large mixer bowl. Stir to dissolve yeast. Add the salt, sugar, oil and almost all of the flour and mix, using the dough hook and a low speed, until the dough comes together and leaves the sides and bottom of the bowl. Knead for three minutes, adding the extra flour if necessary. Knead by hand on a lightly floured board for one minute or until the dough is no longer sticky.

BY FOOD PROCESSOR
PLACE THE YEAST and water in the food processor bowl fitted with the steel blade. Pulse for ten seconds to mix. Add the salt, sugar, oil and almost all of the flour and process, with several pulses to mix, for about one minute. Add enough of the remaining flour so that the dough comes together. Knead by hand on a lightly floured board for one minute or until the dough is no longer sticky.

If you have a small food processor, process the dough in two batches and do not overwork dough.

THE NEXT STEP

PLACE THE DOUGH in a lightly oiled bowl and turn the dough over so that it is very thinly coated all over with oil. Put the bowl in a large plastic bag and leave in a warm place until the dough has doubled in size.

PUNCH DOWN and knead for 10 seconds so that the dough is back to its original size. Shape and use as required.

FOR BREAD BAKED IN A PAN

LIGHTLY GREASE a deep 22 x 12 cm (9 x 5 in) pan with butter or margarine. Flatten the dough into a 1 cm (½ in) thick oval and roll up. Pinch the ends together and place with the smooth side uppermost in the greased pan. Cover with a dry cloth and leave the dough until it rises to the top of the pan.

PREHEAT OVEN to hot (220°C/425°F).

SPRAY OR BRUSH with water or milk glaze. Bake for 15 minutes, then reduce the heat to moderate (180°C/350°F). Bake for a further 20 minutes or until the bread sounds hollow when tapped on the bottom and there is no stale beer smell. Turn out of the pan and cool on a wire rack. For a soft crust cover loosely with a cloth.

This simple bread is good to eat just as it is or you can change it by adding extras. Try herbs or a spoonful of tomato paste or chopped onion or anything you like the sound of.

Plain Wholemeal Bread

20 g (¾ oz) fresh yeast or
  1 sachet dried yeast
1½ cups water, lukewarm
  for fresh yeast, warm for
  dried yeast
2 level teaspoons salt
2 level teaspoons brown sugar
1 tablespoon oil or melted
  butter
2 cups wholemeal (whole-
  wheat) flour
1½ to 2 cups bread making
  flour or plain (all-purpose)
  flour sifted with 3 level
  teaspoons gluten flour

GLAZE
water or milk

BY HAND

PLACE THE YEAST in a large mixing bowl, add the water and stir until the yeast softens and dissolves a little. Add the salt, sugar, oil and half of the flour and beat very well with a strong wooden spoon. Add almost all of the remaining flour, a half a cupful at a time. When the dough becomes too hard to work with the spoon, use just one floured hand to knead the dough in the bowl.

TURN THE DOUGH onto a lightly floured board and knead for five minutes or until the dough no longer sticks to your hands or the board and it is smooth and elastic. Use just a very light sprinkling of flour on the board to stop the dough from sticking.

BY MIXER

PLACE THE YEAST and water in a large mixer bowl. Stir to dissolve yeast. Add the salt, sugar, oil and almost all of the flour and mix, using the dough hook and a low speed, until the dough comes together and leaves the sides and bottom of the bowl. Knead for three minutes, adding the extra flour if necessary. Knead by hand on a lightly floured board for one minute or until the dough is no longer sticky.

BY FOOD PROCESSOR

PLACE THE YEAST and water in the food processor bowl fitted with the steel blade. Pulse for 10 seconds to mix. Add the salt, sugar, oil and almost all of the flour and process, with several pulses to mix, for about one minute. Add enough of the remaining flour so that the dough comes together. Knead by hand on a lightly floured board for one minute or until the dough is no longer sticky.

If you have a small food processor, process the dough in two batches and do not overwork dough.

THE NEXT STEP

PLACE THE DOUGH in a lightly oiled bowl and turn dough over so that it is very thinly coated all over with oil. Put the bowl in a large plastic bag and leave in a warm place until the dough has doubled in size.

PUNCH DOWN and knead for 10 seconds so that the dough is back to its original size. Flatten the dough into a 1 cm (½ in) thick oval and roll up. Pinch the ends together and place with the smooth side uppermost in a deep greased 22 x 12 cm (9 x 5 in) pan. Cover with a dry cloth and leave the dough until it rises to the top of the pan.

PREHEAT OVEN to hot (220°C/425°F).

SPRAY OR BRUSH the dough with water or milk. Bake for 15 minutes, then reduce the heat to moderate (180°C/350°F). Bake for a further 20 minutes or until the bread sounds hollow when tapped on the bottom and there is no stale beer smell. Turn out of the pan and cool on a wire rack.

You can use all wholemeal flour in this bread if you want to, but the addition of the other flour makes the loaf lighter and higher.

Rich Wholemeal Bread

2 cups boiling water
1 cup cracked wheat
30 g (1 oz) fresh yeast or
  1½ sachets dried yeast
2 level teaspoons salt
2 tablespoons light honey
2 tablespoons oil or melted
  butter
1 egg, lightly beaten
2 level tablespoons soy flour
2 cups wholemeal (whole-
  wheat) flour
1 to 1½ cups bread making
  flour or plain (all-purpose)
  flour sifted with 1 level
  teaspoon gluten flour

GLAZE
extra melted butter

Pour the boiling water over the cracked wheat grains and leave to cool to lukewarm for fresh yeast and warm for dried yeast. Drain the grain and re-measure water. Add more water if needed to make up to 1½ cups.

BY HAND

PLACE THE YEAST in a large mixing bowl, add the water and stir until the yeast dissolves. Add the salt, honey, oil, soaked cracked wheat, beaten egg, soy flour and the wholemeal flour and beat very well with a wooden spoon. Add almost all of the bread making flour, a half a cupful at a time. When the dough becomes too stiff for the spoon, use just one floured hand to knead the dough in the bowl.

TURN THE DOUGH onto a lightly floured board and knead for five minutes or until the dough no longer sticks to your hands or the board and the dough is smooth and elastic. Use just a very light sprinkling of flour on the board to stop the dough from sticking.

BY MIXER

PLACE THE YEAST and water in a large mixer bowl. Stir to dissolve yeast. Add the salt, honey, oil, soaked cracked wheat, beaten egg, soy flour, wholemeal flour and almost all of the bread making flour and mix, using the dough hook and a low speed, until the dough comes together and leaves the sides and bottom of the bowl. Knead for three minutes, adding the extra flour if necessary. Knead by hand on a lightly floured board for one minute or until the dough is no longer sticky.

BY FOOD PROCESSOR

PLACE THE YEAST and water in the food processor bowl fitted with the steel blade. Pulse for 10 seconds to mix. Add the salt, honey, oil, soaked cracked wheat, beaten egg, soy flour, wholemeal flour and almost all of the bread making flour and process, with several pulses to mix, for about one minute. Add enough of the remaining flour so that the dough comes together. Knead by hand on a lightly floured board for one minute or until the dough is no longer sticky.

If you have a small food processor, process the dough in two batches and do not overwork dough.

THE NEXT STEP

PLACE THE DOUGH in a lightly oiled bowl and turn the dough over so it is thinly coated on all sides with oil. Put the bowl in a large plastic bag in a warm place until the dough has doubled in size.

PUNCH DOWN and knead for 10 seconds so that the dough is back to its original size. Flatten into a 1 cm (½ in) thick oval and roll up tightly. Make shallow slashes along the top and place on a greased baking tray. Cover with a dry cloth and leave to rise until nearly doubled in size.

PREHEAT OVEN to moderately hot (200°C/400°F).

BAKE FOR 35 to 40 minutes or until the bread sounds hollow when tapped on the bottom and there is no stale beer smell. Brush with the extra melted butter and cool on a wire rack.

Many people don't like the strong distinctive taste of protein rich soy flour so use it only sparingly (unless you really love it). It can be useful if you are running out of time as doughs with soy flour can be shaped immediately after mixing and baked after just the one rising.

Beer Bread

20 g (¾ oz) fresh yeast or
  1 sachet dried yeast
1½ cups flat warm beer
1 level teaspoon salt
1 tablespoon raw sugar
1 tablespoon oil or melted
  butter
3½ to 4 cups wholemeal
  (whole-wheat) flour

GLAZE AND DECORATION
water
sesame seeds

BY HAND

PLACE THE YEAST in a large mixing bowl, add the beer and stir until the yeast dissolves. Add the salt, sugar, oil, half the flour and beat very well with a wooden spoon. Add almost all of the remaining flour, a half a cupful at a time. When the dough becomes too stiff for the spoon, use just one floured hand to knead the dough in the bowl.

TURN THE DOUGH onto a lightly floured board and knead for five minutes or until the dough no longer sticks to your hands or the board and the dough is smooth and elastic. Use just a very light sprinkling of flour on the board to stop the dough from sticking. Place the dough in a lightly oiled bowl and turn dough over so that it is thinly coated on all sides with oil.

BY MIXER

PLACE THE YEAST and beer in a large mixer bowl. Stir to dissolve yeast. Add the remaining ingredients and almost all of the flour and mix, using the dough hook and a low speed, until the dough comes together and leaves the sides and bottom of the bowl. Knead for three minutes, adding the extra flour if necessary. Knead by hand on a lightly floured board for one minute or until the dough is no longer sticky.

BY FOOD PROCESSOR

PLACE THE YEAST and beer in the food processor bowl fitted with the steel blade. Pulse for ten seconds to mix. Add the remaining ingredients and almost all of the flour and process, with several pulses to mix, for about one minute. Add enough of the remaining flour so that the dough comes together. Knead by hand on a lightly floured board for one minute or until the dough is no longer sticky.

If you have a small food processor, process the dough in two batches and do not overwork dough.

THE NEXT STEP

PUT THE BOWL in a large plastic bag and leave in a warm place until the dough has doubled in size.

PUNCH DOWN and knead for 10 seconds so that the dough is back to its original size. Shape into a round and place on a greased baking tray, cover with a dry cloth and leave to rise until nearly doubled in size.

PREHEAT OVEN to moderately hot (200°C/400°F).

SPRAY LIGHTLY with water and dust with sesame seeds. Bake for 35 to 40 minutes or until the bread sounds hollow when tapped on the bottom and there is no stale beer smell. Cool on a wire rack.

The beer does not have to be flat for this bread. You can use freshly opened beer if the beer drinkers will let you.

Raisin Loaf

20 g (¾ oz) fresh yeast or
    1 sachet dried yeast
1¼ cups water, lukewarm
    for fresh yeast, warm for
    dried yeast
¼ level teaspoon salt
¼ cup sugar
2 tablespoons melted butter
    or oil
½ level teaspoon ground
    cinnamon
½ level teaspoon ground
    nutmeg
3½ to 4 cups bread making
    flour or plain (all-purpose)
    flour sifted with 3 level
    teaspoons gluten flour
1 cup raisins or sultanas
    (golden raisins)
½ cup mixed peel (candied
    orange and lemon)

BY HAND

PLACE THE YEAST in a large mixing bowl, add the water and stir until the yeast dissolves. Add the salt, sugar, melted butter, ground cinnamon, ground nutmeg and half of the flour and beat very well with a wooden spoon. Add almost all of the remaining flour, a half a cupful at a time. When the dough becomes too stiff for the spoon, use just one floured hand to knead the dough in the bowl.

TURN THE DOUGH onto a lightly floured board and knead for five minutes or until the dough no longer sticks to your hands or the board and it is smooth and elastic. Use just a very light sprinkling of flour on the board to stop the dough from sticking.

BY MIXER

PLACE THE YEAST and water in a large mixer bowl. Stir to dissolve yeast. Add the remaining ingredients (except the raisins and mixed peel) and almost all of the flour. Mix, using the dough hook and a low speed, until the dough comes together and leaves the sides and bottom of the bowl. Knead for three minutes, adding the extra flour if necessary. Knead by hand on a lightly floured board for one minute or until the dough is no longer sticky.

Glaze
¼ cup water mixed with 2 teaspoons sugar

BY FOOD PROCESSOR

PLACE THE YEAST and water in the food processor bowl fitted with the steel blade. Pulse for ten seconds to mix. Add the remaining ingredients (except the raisins and mixed peel) and almost all of the flour. Process, with several pulses to mix, for about one minute. Add enough of the remaining flour so that the dough comes together. Knead by hand on a lightly floured board for one minute or until the dough is no longer sticky.

If you have a small food processor, process the dough in two batches and do not overwork dough.

THE NEXT STEP

PLACE THE DOUGH in a lightly oiled bowl and turn dough over so that it is very thinly coated all over with oil. Put the bowl in a large plastic bag and leave in a warm place until the dough has doubled in size.

PUNCH DOWN and knead for 10 seconds so that the dough is back to its original size. Knead in the raisins and mixed peel. Flatten the dough into a 1 cm (½ in) thick oval and roll up like a Swiss (jelly) roll. Pinch the ends together and place with the smooth side uppermost in a deep greased 22 x 12 cm (9 x 5 in) pan. Cover with a dry cloth and leave the dough until it rises to the top of the pan.

PREHEAT OVEN to moderate (180°C/350°F).

BRUSH LIGHTLY with the water and sugar glaze. Bake for 40 to 50 minutes or until the bread sounds hollow when tapped on the bottom and there is no stale beer smell. Turn out of the pan and cool on a wire rack.

I really prefer to shape breads into freestanding rounds or loaves but I always think that Raisin Loaf must be baked in a pan because that's the way I've been eating my raisin toast since I was little.

Multigrain Bread

20 g (¾ oz) fresh yeast or
   1 sachet dried yeast
1½ cups water, lukewarm
   for fresh yeast, warm for
   dried yeast
1 level teaspoon salt
1 level tablespoon brown
   sugar
2 tablespoons oil
2 cups wholemeal (whole-
   wheat) flour
1½ to 2 cups bread making
   flour or plain (all-purpose)
   flour sifted with 2 level
   teaspoons gluten flour
½ cup cooked wheat grains
½ cup cooked rye grains
½ cup cooked brown rice

GLAZE AND DECORATION
water
extra cooked grains

BY HAND

PLACE THE YEAST in a large mixing bowl, add the water and stir until the yeast dissolves. Add the salt, sugar, oil and half of each flour and beat very well with a wooden spoon. Add almost all of the remaining flour, a half a cupful at a time. When the dough becomes too stiff for the spoon, use just one floured hand to knead the dough in the bowl.

TURN THE DOUGH onto a lightly floured board and knead for five minutes or until the dough no longer sticks to your hands or the board and it is smooth and elastic. Use just a very light sprinkling of flour on the board to stop the dough from sticking.

BY MIXER

PLACE THE YEAST and water in a large mixer bowl. Stir to dissolve yeast. Add the salt, sugar, oil, wholemeal flour and almost all of the bread making flour and mix, using the dough hook and a low speed, until the dough comes together and leaves the sides and bottom of the bowl. Knead for three minutes, adding the extra flour if necessary. Knead by hand on a lightly floured board for one minute or until the dough is no longer sticky.

BY FOOD PROCESSOR

PLACE THE YEAST and water in the food processor bowl fitted with the steel blade. Pulse for 10 seconds to mix. Add the salt, sugar, oil, wholemeal flour and almost all of the bread making flour and process, with several pulses to mix, for about one minute. Add enough of the remaining flour so that the dough comes together. Knead by hand on a lightly floured board for one minute or until the dough is no longer sticky.

If you have a small food processor, process the dough in two batches and do not overwork dough.

THE NEXT STEP

PLACE THE DOUGH in a lightly oiled bowl and turn dough over so that it is very thinly coated all over with oil. Put the bowl in a large plastic bag and leave in a warm place until the dough has doubled in size.

ADD THE COOKED GRAINS and rice. Punch down and knead until the grains and rice are mixed through the dough. Cover with a cloth and leave for five minutes. Flatten the dough into a 1 cm (½ in) thick oval and roll up. Pinch the ends together and place with the smooth side uppermost in a 22 x 12 cm (9 x 5 in) deep greased pan. Cover with a dry cloth and leave the dough until it rises to the top of the pan.

PREHEAT OVEN to moderately hot (200°C/400°F).

SPRAY OR BRUSH lightly with water and sprinkle on the extra cooked grains. Bake for 35 to 40 minutes, or until the bread sounds hollow when tapped on the bottom and there is no stale beer smell. Turn out of the pan and cool on a wire rack.

Always cook any whole grains before using them in your doughs. If you think you can avoid this step it's clear you haven't damaged a tooth on undercooked or raw grains.

Buttermilk Plait

30 g (1 oz) fresh yeast or
  1½ sachets dried yeast
¼ cup water, lukewarm for
  fresh yeast, warm for dried
  yeast
1 cup buttermilk, at room
  temperature
1 level teaspoon salt
2 level tablespoons soft
  brown sugar
3½ to 4 cups bread making
  flour or plain (all-purpose)
  flour sifted with 3 level
  teaspoons gluten flour

GLAZE AND DECORATION
extra buttermilk
poppyseeds or sesame seeds

BY HAND
PLACE THE YEAST in a large mixing bowl, add the water and stir until the yeast dissolves. Add the buttermilk, salt, sugar, and half of the flour and beat very well with a wooden spoon. Add almost all of the remaining flour, a half a cupful at a time. When the dough becomes too stiff for the spoon, use just one floured hand to knead the dough in the bowl.

TURN THE DOUGH onto a lightly floured board and knead for five minutes or until the dough no longer sticks to your hands or the board and it is smooth and elastic. Use just a very light sprinkling of flour on the board to stop the dough from sticking.

BY MIXER
PLACE THE YEAST and water in a large mixer bowl. Stir to dissolve yeast. Add the remaining ingredients and almost all of the flour and mix, using the dough hook and a low speed, until the dough comes together and leaves the sides and bottom of the bowl. Knead for three minutes, adding the extra flour if necessary. Knead by hand on a lightly floured board for one minute or until the dough is no longer sticky.

BY FOOD PROCESSOR
PLACE THE YEAST and water in the food processor bowl fitted with the steel blade. Pulse for 10 seconds to mix. Add the remaining ingredients and almost all of the flour and process, with several pulses to mix, for about one minute. Add enough of the remaining flour so that the dough comes together. Knead by hand on a lightly floured board for one minute or until the dough is no longer sticky.

If you have a small food processor, process the dough in two batches and do not overwork dough.

THE NEXT STEP

PLACE THE DOUGH in a lightly oiled bowl and turn dough over so that it is very thinly coated all over with oil. Put the bowl in a large plastic bag and leave in a warm place until the dough has doubled in size.

PUNCH DOWN and knead for 10 seconds so that the dough is back to its original size. Divide the dough into three, cover and leave for five minutes.

ROLL, SQUEEZE AND STRETCH dough into long strands on a lightly floured surface. Place the strands onto a greased baking tray and plait (braid). Cover with a dry cloth and leave to rise until nearly doubled in size.

PREHEAT OVEN to moderately hot (200°C/400°F).

SPRAY WITH WATER and sprinkle on poppyseeds or sesame seeds.

BAKE FOR 40 to 45 minutes or until the bread sounds hollow when tapped on the bottom and there is nop stale beer smell. Cool on the rack.

I can only manage to plait (braid) three strands of dough, but if you can do more, astonish and impress everyone (I've met rare people who plait six and I've heard of one who could do eight.

Cheese Bread

30 g (1 oz) fresh yeast or
  1½ sachets dried yeast
1¼ cups water, lukewarm
  for fresh yeast, warm for
  dried yeast
2 level teaspoons salt
2 level teaspoons sugar
2 tablespoons oil or melted
  butter
¼ cup finely grated fresh
  parmesan cheese
½ cup grated sharp
  cheddar cheese
3½ to 4 cups bread making
  flour or plain (all-purpose)
  flour sifted with 3 level
  teaspoons gluten flour

GLAZE AND DECORATION
milk
extra grated cheese

BY HAND

PLACE THE YEAST in a large mixing bowl, add the water and stir until the yeast dissolves. Add the salt, sugar, oil, cheese and half of the flour and beat very well with a wooden spoon. Add almost all of the remaining flour, a half a cupful at a time. When the dough becomes too stiff for the spoon, use just one floured hand to knead the dough in the bowl.

TURN THE DOUGH onto a lightly floured board and knead for five minutes or until the dough no longer sticks to your hands or the board and it is elastic. Use just a very light sprinkling of flour on the board to stop the dough from sticking.

BY MIXER

PLACE THE YEAST and water in a large mixer bowl. Stir to dissolve yeast. Add the remaining ingredients and almost all of the flour and mix, using the dough hook and a low speed, until the dough comes together and leaves the sides and bottom of the bowl. Knead for three

RIGHT: Simple Plain White Bread (page 23)

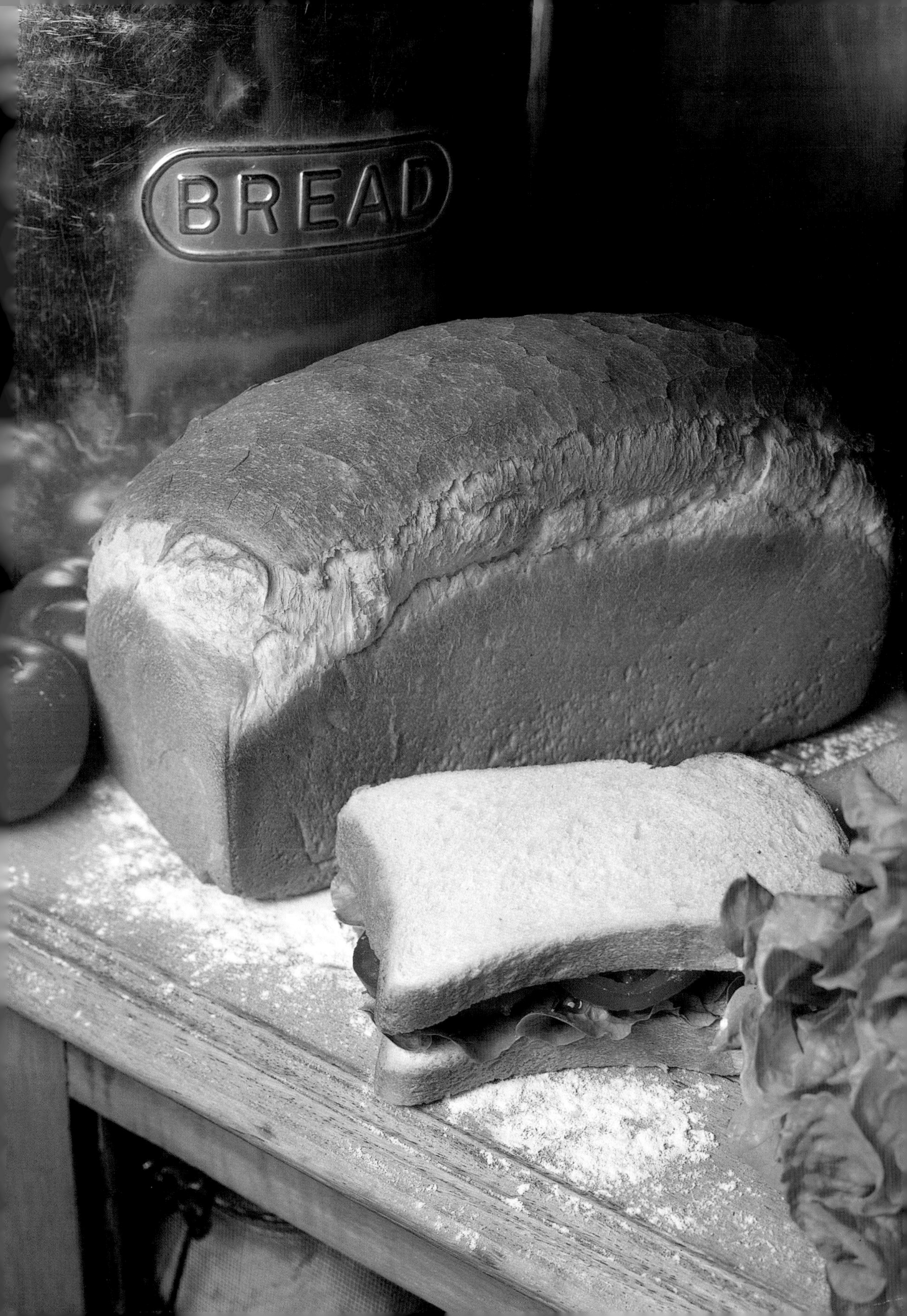
BREAD

minutes, adding the extra flour if necessary. Knead by hand on a lightly floured board for one minute or until the dough is no longer sticky.

BY FOOD PROCESSOR

PLACE THE YEAST and water in the food processor bowl fitted with the steel blade. Pulse for 10 seconds to mix. Add the remaining ingredients and almost all of the flour and process, with several pulses to mix, for about one minute. Add enough of the remaining flour so that the dough comes together. Knead by hand on a lightly floured board for one minute or until the dough is no longer sticky.

If you have a small food processor, process the dough in two batches and do not overwork dough.

THE NEXT STEP

PLACE THE DOUGH in a lightly oiled bowl and turn dough over so that it is very thinly coated all over with oil. Put the bowl in a large plastic bag and leave in a warm place until the dough has doubled in size. **PUNCH DOWN** and knead for 10 seconds so that the dough is back to its original size. Flatten the dough into a 1 cm (½ in) thick oval and roll up. Pinch the ends together and place with the smooth side uppermost in a deep greased 22 x 12 cm (9 x 5 in) pan. Cover with a dry cloth and leave the dough until it rises to the top of the pan. **PREHEAT OVEN** to hot (220°C/425°F).
BRUSH OR SPRAY lightly with milk and sprinkle on the extra cheese. **BAKE FOR** 15 minutes, then reduce the heat to moderate (180°C/ 350°F). Bake for a further 20 minutes or until the bread sounds hollow when tapped on the bottom and there is no stale beer smell. Turn out of the pan and cool on a wire rack.

You can vary this bread by adding small cubes of ham, or lightly fried chopped bacon and sautéed chopped onions would be good too.

Light Rye Bread

20 g (¾ oz) fresh yeast or
  1 sachet dried yeast
1½ cups water, lukewarm
  for fresh yeast, warm for
  dried yeast
1 level teaspoon salt
1 teaspoon brown sugar or
  molasses
2 teaspoons oil
2 teaspoons caraway seeds
1 cup rye flour

BY HAND

PLACE THE YEAST in a large mixing bowl, add the water and stir until the yeast dissolves. Add the salt, sugar, oil, caraway seeds, rye and wholemeal flours and beat very well with a wooden spoon. Add almost all of the remaining flour, a half a cupful at a time. When the dough becomes too stiff for the spoon, use just one floured hand to knead the dough in the bowl.
TURN THE DOUGH onto a lightly floured board and knead for five

LEFT: *Poppyseed Baguettes (page 42)*

1½ cups wholemeal flour
1 to 1½ cups bread making
  flour or plain (all-
  purpose) flour sifted with
  2 level teaspoons gluten
  flour

GLAZE
cold black coffee

minutes or until the dough no longer sticks to your hands or the board and the dough is smooth and elastic. Use just a very light sprinkling of flour on the board to stop the dough from sticking.

BY MIXER

PLACE THE YEAST and water in a large mixer bowl. Stir to dissolve yeast. Add the remaining ingredients and almost all of the bread making flour and mix, using the dough hook and a low speed, until the dough comes together and leaves the sides and bottom of the bowl. Knead for three minutes, adding the extra flour if necessary. Knead by hand on a lightly floured board for one minute or until the dough is no longer sticky.

BY FOOD PROCESSOR

Place the yeast and water in the food processor bowl fitted with the steel blade. Pulse for 10 seconds to mix. Add the remaining ingredients and almost all of the bread making flour and process, with several pulses to mix, for about one minute. Add enough of the remaining flour so that the dough comes together. Knead by hand on a lightly floured board for one minute or until the dough is no longer sticky.

If you have a small food processor, process the dough in two batches and do not overwork dough.

THE NEXT STEP

PLACE THE DOUGH in a lightly oiled bowl and turn dough over so that it is thinly coated on all sides with oil. Put the bowl in a large plastic bag and leave in a warm place until the dough has doubled in size.

PUNCH DOWN and knead for 10 seconds so that the dough is back to its original size. Flatten the bread into a 1 cm (½ in) thick oval and roll up like a Swiss (jelly) roll to make a log shape. Cover with a dry cloth and leave to rise until nearly doubled in size again.

PREHEAT OVEN to moderately hot (200°C/400°F).

BRUSH LIGHTLY with cold black coffee and bake for 35 to 40 minutes or until the bread sounds hollow when tapped on the bottom and there is no stale beer smell. Cool on a wire rack.

If you started your bread making with a rye dough you may have been put off kneading for life as rye doughs don't have the same nice feel as wheat flour doughs. People often really don't like the clay-like feel but it's always worth the effort for the great taste of rye bread.

Dark Rye Bread

1 ¾ cups boiling water

1 cup kibbled (cracked) rye grains

30 g (1 oz) fresh yeast or 1½ sachets dried yeast

1 level teaspoon salt

2 tablespoons treacle

2 tablespoons oil or melted butter

½ level teaspoon instant coffee powder

1 level tablespoon cocoa powder

2 teaspoons caraway seeds

¼ teaspoon ground fennel

½ cup bran cereal

1 tablespoon vinegar

1½ cups rye flour

1 cup wholemeal (whole-wheat) flour

1 to 1½ cups bread making flour or plain (all-purpose) flour sifted with 1 level teaspoon gluten flour

Pour the boiling water over the kibbled rye grains and leave to cool to lukewarm for fresh yeast and warm for dried yeast. Drain the grain and re-measure water. Add more water if needed to make up to 1½ cups.

BY HAND

PLACE THE YEAST in a large mixing bowl, add the water and stir until the yeast dissolves.

ADD THE SOAKED GRAINS, salt, treacle, oil, instant coffee powder, cocoa powder, caraway seeds, ground fennel, bran cereal, vinegar and the rye and wholemeal flours. Beat very well with a wooden spoon. Add almost all of the remaining flour, a half a cupful at a time. When the dough becomes too stiff for the spoon, use just one floured hand to knead the dough in the bowl.

TURN THE DOUGH onto a lightly floured board and knead for five minutes or until the dough no longer sticks to your hands or the board and it is smooth and elastic. Use just a very light sprinkling of flour on the board to stop the dough from sticking.

BY MIXER

PLACE THE YEAST and water in a large mixer bowl. Stir to dissolve yeast. Add the soaked grains, salt, treacle, oil, instant coffee powder, cocoa powder, caraway seeds, ground fennel, bran cereal, vinegar, rye flour, wholemeal flour and almost all of the bread making flour and mix, using the dough hook and a low speed, until the dough comes together and leaves the sides and bottom of the bowl. Knead for three minutes, adding the extra flour if necessary. Knead by hand on a lightly floured board for one minute or until the dough is no longer sticky.

BY FOOD PROCESSOR

PLACE THE YEAST and water in the food processor bowl fitted with the steel blade. Pulse for 10 seconds to mix. Add the soaked grains, salt, treacle, oil, instant coffee powder, cocoa powder, caraway seeds, ground fennel, bran cereal, vinegar, rye flour, wholemeal flour and almost all of the bread making flour and process, with several pulses to mix, for about one minute. Add enough of the remaining flour so that the dough comes together. Knead by hand on a lightly floured board for one minute or until the dough is no longer sticky.

If you have a small food processor, process the dough in two batches and do not overwork dough.

THE NEXT STEP

PLACE THE DOUGH in a lightly oiled bowl and turn dough over so that it is very thinly coated all over with oil. Put the bowl in a large plastic bag and leave in a warm place until the dough has doubled in size.

PUNCH DOWN and knead for 30 seconds so that the dough is back to its original size. Flatten the bread into an oval shape and roll up like a Swiss (jelly) roll to make a log shape. Place on a greased tray and cover with a dry cloth. Leave to rise until nearly doubled in size again.

PREHEAT OVEN to moderately hot (200°C/400°F).

MAKE SHALLOW CUTS along the bread with a very sharp knife or a single edged razor blade. Bake for 45 to 50 minutes or until the bread sounds hollow when tapped on the bottom and there is no stale beer smell. Cool on a wire rack.

This is a really dark heavy bread and you may find it takes longer to rise than other doughs. It can't really claim to be a truly traditional rye bread, not with the instant coffee and the bran cereal, but it has a great taste and most adults, and occasionally children, like it.

Swedish Rye Bread

*30 g (1 oz) fresh yeast or
1½ sachets dried yeast
1½ cups water, lukewarm
for fresh yeast, warm for
dried yeast
2 level teaspoons salt
¹/₃ cup molasses
2 tablespoons oil or melted
butter
1 level teaspoon fennel seeds
1 level teaspoon cumin seeds
2 level teaspoons grated
orange rind
2 cups rye flour
1½ to 2 cups bread making
flour or plain (all-purpose)
flour sifted with 2 level
teaspoons gluten flour*

*GLAZE
1 level teaspoon instant
coffee mixed in a little water*

The seeds, orange rind and molasses make this bread extremely dark, rich and flavoursome.

BY HAND

PLACE THE YEAST in a large mixing bowl, add the water and stir until the yeast dissolves. Add the salt, molasses, oil, seeds, orange rind and the rye flour and beat very well with a wooden spoon. Add almost all of the remaining flour, a half a cupful at a time. When the dough becomes too stiff for the spoon, use just one floured hand to knead the dough in the bowl.

TURN ONTO a lightly floured board and knead for five minutes or until the dough no longer sticks to your hands or the board and it is smooth and elastic. Use just a very light sprinkling of flour on the board to stop the dough from sticking.

BY MIXER

PLACE THE YEAST and water in a large mixer bowl. Stir to dissolve yeast. Add the remaining ingredients and almost all of the bread making flour and mix, using the dough hook and a low speed, until the dough comes together and leaves the sides and bottom of the bowl. Knead for three minutes, adding the extra flour if

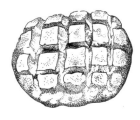

necessary. Knead by hand on a lightly floured board for one minute or until the dough is no longer sticky.

BY FOOD PROCESSOR

PLACE THE YEAST and water in the food processor bowl fitted with the steel blade. Pulse for 10 seconds to mix. Add the remaining ingredients and almost all of the bread making flour and process, with several pulses to mix, for about one minute. Add enough of the remaining flour so that the dough comes together. Knead by hand on a lightly floured board for one minute or until the dough is no longer sticky.

If you only have a small food processor, process the dough in two batches and do not overwork dough.

THE NEXT STEP

PLACE THE DOUGH in a lightly oiled bowl and turn dough over so that it is very thinly coated all over with oil. Put the bowl in a large plastic bag and leave in a warm place until the dough has doubled in size.

PUNCH DOWN and knead for 10 seconds so that the dough is back to its original size. Divide the dough in half and shape each into a round, slightly flat loaf. Place on a greased baking tray, cover with a dry cloth and allow to rise until doubled in size again.

PREHEAT OVEN to moderately hot (200°C/400°F).

CUT A CRISSCROSS pattern on top of the loaves with a single edged razor blade or a thin sharp knife. Brush lightly with the instant coffee glaze. Bake for 30 to 35 minutes or until the loaves sound hollow when tapped on the bottom and there is no stale beer smell. Cool on a wire rack.

Vienna Bread

20 g (¾ oz) fresh yeast or
   1 sachet dried yeast
½ cup water, lukewarm for
   fresh yeast, warm for dried
   yeast
¾ cup milk
1 level teaspoon salt
1 level teaspoon sugar
1 teaspoon oil
1 egg white, lightly beaten
3½ to 4 cups bread making
   flour or plain (all-
   purpose) flour sifted with
   3 level teaspoons gluten
   flour
cornmeal (polenta) for the
   baking tray

GLAZE AND DECORATION
1 egg white, lightly beaten
poppyseeds or sesame seeds

BY HAND

PLACE THE YEAST in a large mixing bowl, add the water and stir until the yeast dissolves. Add the milk, salt, sugar, oil, egg white and half of the flour and beat very well with a wooden spoon. Add almost all of the remaining flour, a half a cupful at a time. When the dough becomes too stiff for the spoon, use just one floured hand to knead the dough in the bowl.

TURN THE DOUGH onto a lightly floured board and knead for five minutes or until the dough no longer sticks to your hands or the board and it is smooth and elastic. Use just a very light sprinkling of flour on the board to stop the dough from sticking.

BY MIXER

PLACE THE YEAST and water in a large mixer bowl. Stir to dissolve yeast. Add the remaining ingredients and almost all of the flour and mix, using the dough hook and a low speed, until the dough comes together and leaves the sides and bottom of the bowl. Knead for three minutes, adding the extra flour if necessary. Knead by hand on a lightly floured board for one minute or until the dough is no longer sticky.

BY FOOD PROCESSOR

PLACE THE YEAST and water in the food processor bowl fitted with the steel blade. Pulse for 10 seconds to mix. Add the remaining ingredients and almost all of the flour and process, with several pulses to mix, for about one minute. Add enough of the remaining flour so that the dough comes together. Knead by hand on a lightly floured board for one minute or until the dough is no longer sticky.

If you have a small food processor, process the dough in two batches and do not overwork dough.

THE NEXT STEP

PLACE THE DOUGH in a lightly oiled bowl and turn dough over so that it is very thinly coated all over with oil. Put the bowl in a large plastic bag and leave in a warm place until the dough has doubled in size.

PUNCH DOWN and knead for 10 seconds so that the dough is back to its original size. Flatten the dough into a large oval and roll up from a long side into a tight roll. Lightly grease a baking tray and spread the cornmeal thickly in the centre. Place the shaped loaf on top of the cornmeal and cover with a dry cloth. Leave to rise until nearly doubled in size again.

PREHEAT OVEN to hot (220°C/425°F).

BRUSH VERY LIGHTLY with the extra egg white and sprinkle with the seeds. Make a slash with a very thin sharp knife or a single edged razor blade along the loaf. Bake in for 30 to 35 minutes or until the loaf sounds hollow when tapped on the bottom and there is no stale beer smell. Spray with water after the first three minutes, of baking, again in another three minutes, and, for a final time, three minutes, later. Cool on a wire rack.

You use cornmeal (or polenta) on the baking tray to make the crust that is on the bottom really crisp. Dried breadcrumbs will have much the same effect, but will lack the crunch of the cornmeal.

Traditional French Bread

10 g (¹/₃ oz) fresh yeast or ½ sachet dried yeast
1¼ cups water, lukewarm for fresh yeast, warm for dried yeast
2 level teaspoons salt
3½ to 4 cups bread making or plain (all-purpose) flour sifted with 3 level teaspoons gluten flour

BY HAND

PLACE THE YEAST in a large mixing bowl, add the water and stir until the yeast dissolves. Add the salt and half of the flour and beat very well with a wooden spoon. Add almost all of the remaining flour, a half a cupful at a time. When the dough becomes too stiff for the spoon, use just one floured hand to knead the dough in the bowl.
TURN ONTO a lightly floured board and knead for five minutes or until the dough no longer sticks to your hands or the board and it is smooth and elastic. Use just a very light sprinkling of flour on the board to stop the dough from sticking.

BY MIXER

PLACE THE YEAST and water in a large mixer bowl. Stir to dissolve yeast. Add the salt and almost all of the flour and mix, using the dough hook and a low speed, until the dough comes together and leaves the sides and bottom of the bowl. Knead for three minutes, adding the extra flour if necessary. Knead by hand on a lightly floured board for one minute or until the dough is no longer sticky.

BY FOOD PROCESSOR

PLACE THE YEAST and water in the food processor bowl fitted with the steel blade. Pulse for 10 seconds to mix. Add the salt and almost all of the flour and process, with several pulses to mix, for about one minute. Add enough of the remaining flour so that the dough comes together. Knead by hand on a lightly floured board for one minute or until the dough is no longer sticky.

If you only have a small food processor, process the dough in two batches and do not overwork dough.

THE NEXT STEP

PLACE THE DOUGH in a lightly oiled bowl and turn dough over so that it is very thinly coated all over with oil. Put the bowl in a large plastic bag and leave in a cool place until the dough has doubled in size. A cool place is slower but provides a much better flavour.

PUNCH DOWN and knead for 10 seconds so that the dough is back to its original size. Put the dough back into the bowl and then into the plastic bag and leave it in a cool place until the dough has doubled in size again.

PUNCH DOWN and knead for 10 seconds so the dough is back to its original size. Shape, rise and bake as required. (Refer to Shaping and Baking French Bread page 41.)

It's almost possible to duplicate a loaf of plain French bread using the first recipe (Traditional French Bread page 39). The crust will be crisp, the inside will be patterned with holes and the bread will have the body and the very real chewyness of real French bread. The four ingredients in it are the only ones permitted by French law and the only other ingredient you will need is the time that's necessary for the slow rising and maturing of the dough (which gives fabulous flavour to the bread).

All of that traditional business with the water and baking on the quarry tiles helps to make the crust crisp, as does cooling the bread in a draught.

Fast French Bread

20 g (¾ oz) fresh yeast or
  1 sachet dried yeast
1¾ cups water, lukewarm
  for fresh yeast, warm for
  dried yeast
1 level teaspoon salt
1 level teaspoon sugar
3½ to 4 cups bread making
  or plain (all-purpose) flour
  sifted with 3 level teaspoons
  gluten flour

BY HAND

PLACE THE YEAST in a large mixing bowl, add the water and stir until the yeast dissolves. Add the salt, sugar and half of the flour and beat very well with a wooden spoon. Add almost all of the remaining flour, a half a cupful at a time. When the dough becomes too stiff for the spoon, use just one floured hand to knead the dough in the bowl.

TURN ONTO a lightly floured board and knead for five minutes or until the dough no longer sticks to your hands or the board and it is smooth and elastic. Use just a very light sprinkling of flour on the board to stop the dough from sticking.

BY MIXER

PLACE THE YEAST and water in a large mixer bowl. Stir to dissolve yeast. Add the remaining ingredients and almost all of the flour and mix, using the dough hook and a low speed, until the dough comes together and leaves the sides and bottom of the bowl. Knead for three minutes, adding the extra flour if necessary. Knead by hand on a lightly floured board for one minute or until the dough is no longer sticky.

BY FOOD PROCESSOR

PLACE THE YEAST and water in the food processor bowl fitted with the steel blade. Pulse for 10 seconds to mix. Add the remaining ingredients and almost all of the flour and process, with several pulses to mix, for about one minute. Add enough of the remaining flour so that the dough comes together. Knead by hand on a lightly floured board for one minute or until the dough is no longer sticky.

If you only have a small food processor, process the dough in two batches and do not overwork dough.

THE NEXT STEP

PLACE THE DOUGH in a lightly oiled bowl and turn dough over so that it is very thinly coated all over with oil. Put the bowl in a large plastic bag and leave in a warm place until the dough has nearly doubled in size.

PUNCH DOWN and knead for 10 seconds so that the dough is back to its original size. Shape, rise and bake as required. (Refer to Shaping and Baking French Bread below.)

Traditional purists will insist that this is not a true French bread and, of course, they are right. But the addition of extra yeast and a little sugar means everything works faster so you can make, and be eating, this bread in about two hours.

Shaping and Baking French Bread

SMALL BAGUETTES

DIVIDE THE DOUGH into four pieces. Roll each piece into a rectangle 13 x 15 cm (5 x 6 in). Roll up tightly, beginning on a long side, and pinch the edge to seal. Roll ends gently back and forth to taper them.

PLACE LOAVES on a lightly greased baking tray and cover with a dry cloth and leave to rise until nearly doubled in size. Hold a very sharp razor blade almost flat against the bread to make shallow 1.25 cm (½ in) slashes on the top of the loaves.

SPRAY WITH WATER and bake on a layer of unglazed quarry tiles in a hot oven (220°C/425°F) for 20 to 25 minutes or until the bread sounds hollow when tapped on the bottom and there is no stale beer smell. Spray with water after the first three minutes of baking, again in another three minutes and, for a final time, three minutes later. Cool on a wire rack.

POPPYSEED BAGUETTES

DIVIDE THE DOUGH into two. Roll each part into a rectangle 20 x 25 cm (8 x 10 in). Roll up tightly, beginning on a long side, and pinch the edge to seal. Roll the ends gently back and forth to taper them. Place loaves on a lightly greased baking tray and cover with a dry cloth. Leave to rise until nearly doubled in size.

Spray with water and sprinkle lavishly with poppyseeds. Make shallow slashes along the top of the loaf with a sharp thin knife or a single edged razor blade.

BAKE ON A LAYER of unglazed quarry tiles in a hot oven (220°C/ 425°F) for 20 to 25 minutes or until the bread sounds hollow when tapped on the bottom and there is no stale beer smell. Spray with water after the first three minutes of baking, again in another three minutes and, for a final time, three minutes later. Cool on a wire rack.

ROUND ROLLS

DIVIDE THE DOUGH into 10 equal pieces and cover with a cloth. Leave for five minutes and shape into rolls, one at a time, leaving the rest of the dough covered with the cloth.

Place each piece of dough on a lightly floured board and cup your hand over it. Push down hard and rotate your hand until the dough forms into a round. Place the rolls on a lightly greased baking tray and cover with a dry cloth. Leave to rise until nearly doubled in size. Use a cool place for Traditional French bread and a warm place for Fast French bread.

SPRAY WITH WATER and bake on a layer of unglazed quarry tiles in a hot oven (220°C/425°F) for 15 to 20 minutes or until the bread sounds hollow when tapped on the bottom and there is no stale beer smell. Spray with water after the first three minutes, of baking, again in another three minutes, and, for a final time, three minutes, later. Cool on a wire rack.

Speedy Brioche

30 g (1 oz) fresh yeast or
  1½ sachets dried yeast
½ cup water, lukewarm for
  fresh yeast, warm for dried
  yeast
1 level teaspoon salt
1½ level tablespoons sugar
1 cup very soft unsalted
  butter
4 eggs, at room temperature,
  lightly beaten
3½ to 4 cups bread making
  flour or plain (all–purpose)
  flour sifted with 3 level
  teaspoons gluten flour

GLAZE
1 egg yolk
1 teaspoon of water
½ level teaspoon of salt

BY HAND

PLACE THE YEAST in a large mixing bowl, add the water and stir until the yeast dissolves. Add the salt, sugar, butter, eggs and half of the flour and beat very well with a wooden spoon. Add almost all of the remaining flour, a half a cupful at a time. When the dough becomes too stiff for the spoon, use your hands to knead the dough in the bowl for 5 to 10 minutes or until the dough no longer sticks to your hands and is smooth and elastic. Use just a very light sprinkling of flour to stop the dough from sticking. The dough will be very soft.

BY MIXER

PLACE THE YEAST and water in a large mixer bowl. Stir to dissolve yeast. Add the remaining ingredients and almost all of the flour and mix, using the dough hook and a low speed, until the dough comes together and leaves the sides and bottom of the bowl. Knead for three minutes, adding the extra flour if necessary.

BY FOOD PROCESSOR

PLACE THE YEAST and water in the food processor bowl fitted with the steel blade. Pulse for 10 seconds to mix. Add the remaining ingredients and almost all of the flour and process, with several pulses to mix, for about one minute. Add enough of the remaining flour so that the dough comes together.

If you only have a small food processor, process the dough in two batches and do not overwork dough.

THE NEXT STEP

PLACE THE DOUGH in a lightly oiled bowl and turn dough over so that it is very thinly coated all over with oil. Put the bowl in a large plastic bag and leave in a warm place until the dough has doubled in size.

PUNCH DOWN and knead for 10 seconds so that the dough is back to its original size. Shape, rise and bake as required. (Refer to Shaping and Baking Brioche below.)

TO PREPARE the glaze, place all ingredients in a screwtop jar. Put on the lid and shake vigorously to mix.

Shaping and Baking Brioche

BRIOCHE A TETE

DIVIDE THE DOUGH into two equal halves. Pinch off one-fifth of the dough from each half. Shape a larger piece of dough into a round and place in a well greased 20 cm (8 in) fluted brioche pan or a well greased 20 cm (8 in) deep cake pan.

MAKE A deep funnel shaped hole in the centre. Shape one of the smaller pieces of dough into a teardrop shape and place the pointed end into the hole. Repeat with the rest of the dough in another pan. Cover with a dry cloth and let rise in a warm place until the dough has nearly doubled in size.

PREHEAT OVEN to moderately hot (200°C/400°F).

BRUSH LIGHTLY with the glaze taking care not to brush where the two balls of dough join. Bake for 15 minutes. Reduce oven heat to moderate (180°C/350°F) and bake a further 20 to 25 minutes or until a skewer inserted in the middle comes out clean. Turn out of pans and cool on a wire rack.

BABY BRIOCHE

USE HALF-CUP FLUTED brioche moulds and shape, in the same way as for the large Brioche à Tête, using only enough dough to half fill the pans. Cover with a dry cloth and let rise in a warm place until nearly doubled in size.

PREHEAT OVEN to moderately hot (200°C/400°F).

BRUSH LIGHTLY with the glaze taking care not to brush where the two balls of dough join. Bake for 15 to 20 minutes or until a skewer inserted in the middle comes out clean. Turn out of pans and cool on a wire rack.

I was once totally obsessed with making perfectly shaped Brioche à Tête. I worked out the exact amount of dough to use for the topknot; I continually tested ways of placing it in the base; I devised the best glaze of egg yolk and salt for the best browning; and I continually tried to get them to rise evenly in the oven so the topknots went straight up and not to the side. Eventually I decided I was not a machine and would never make machine perfect brioche. My lopsided brioches still tasted wonderful.

Focaccia

*15 g (½ oz) fresh yeast or
  1 sachet dried yeast
1¼ cups water, lukewarm
  for fresh yeast, warm for
  dried yeast
2 level teaspoons salt
2 tablespoons olive oil
3½ to 4 cups bread making
  flour or plain (all-purpose)
  flour sifted with 3 level
  teaspoons gluten flour
2 extra tablespoons olive oil*

BY HAND

PLACE THE YEAST in a large mixing bowl, add the water and stir until the yeast dissolves. Add the salt, olive oil and half of the flour and beat very well with a wooden spoon. Add almost all of the remaining flour, a half a cupful at a time. When the dough becomes too stiff for the spoon, use just one floured hand to knead the dough in the bowl.

TURN THE DOUGH onto a lightly floured board and knead for five minutes or until the dough no longer sticks to your hands or the board and it is smooth and elastic. Use just a very light sprinkling of flour on the board to stop the dough from sticking.

BY MIXER

PLACE THE YEAST and water in a large mixer bowl. Stir to dissolve yeast. Add the salt, olive oil and almost all of the flour and mix, using the dough hook and a low speed, until the dough comes together and leaves the sides and bottom of the bowl. Knead for three minutes, adding the extra flour if necessary. Knead by hand on a lightly floured board for one minute or until the dough is no longer sticky.

BY FOOD PROCESSOR

PLACE THE YEAST and water in the food processor bowl fitted with the steel blade. Pulse for 10 seconds to mix. Add the salt, olive oil and almost all of the flour and process, with several pulses to mix, for about one minute. Add enough of the remaining flour so that the dough comes together. Knead by hand on a lightly floured board for one minute or until the dough is no longer sticky.

If you only have a small food processor, process the dough in two batches and do not overwork dough.

THE NEXT STEP

PLACE THE DOUGH in a lightly oiled bowl and turn dough over so that it is thinly coated all over with oil. Put the bowl in a large plastic bag and leave in a warm place until the dough has doubled in size.

PUNCH DOWN and knead for 10 seconds so that the dough is back to its original size. Place in a greased 25 x 40 cm (10 x 16 in) rectangular pan and flatten with your hands. Cover with a dry cloth and leave to rise until doubled in size; about half the time of the first rising.

POUR ON the extra olive oil and dig your fingertips into the dough

several times to a depth of 1 cm (½ in). Cover with a dry cloth and leave to rise until doubled in size again.

PREHEAT OVEN to moderately hot (200°C/400°F).

BAKE ON a layer of unglazed quarry tiles for about 20 to 25 minutes. Spray with water after the first three minutes, of baking and once again in another three minutes. Turn out of the pan onto a wire rack to cool, with the bottom side uppermost.

Focaccia with Sage

30 fresh sage leaves, chopped
focaccia dough (refer to
  Focaccia recipe, page 45)
1 to 4 level teaspoons salt
whole sage leaves

ADD THE CHOPPED sage leaves to the focaccia dough and prepare for baking as per the Focaccia recipe.

JUST BEFORE BAKING, push the fresh sage leaves down into the dough. Brush the dimpled dough with olive oil and sprinkle with the salt. Bake, spray and cool as per the Focaccia recipe.

Focaccia with Olives

focaccia dough (refer to
  Focaccia recipe, page 45)
250 g (8 oz) black olives,
  stoned

Follow the same directions as for the Focaccia recipe but push the olives into the shaped focaccia just before baking. Bake, spray and cool as per the Focaccia recipe.

Don't think you can substitute any sort of oil for the olive oil. If you do, you end up with bread that doesn't have the flavour of a true Focaccia. I like to use the strongest tasting extra virgin olive oil that I can find as I think it has the best flavour.

Pizza

THE BASE
20 g (¾ oz) fresh yeast or
  1 sachet dried yeast
1¼ cups water, lukewarm
  for fresh yeast, warm for
  dried yeast
2 level teaspoons salt
2 level teaspoons sugar
1 tablespoon olive oil
3½ to 4 cups bread making
  flour or plain flour sifted
  with 3 level teaspoons
  gluten flour

BY HAND

PLACE THE YEAST in a large mixing bowl, add the water and stir until the yeast dissolves. Add the salt, sugar, oil and half of the flour and beat very well with a wooden spoon. Add almost all of the remaining flour, a half a cupful at a time. When the dough becomes too stiff for the spoon, use just one floured hand to knead the dough in the bowl.

TURN THE DOUGH onto a lightly floured board and knead for five minutes or until the dough no longer sticks to your hands or the board and it is smooth and elastic. Use just a very light sprinkling of flour on the board to stop the dough from sticking.

THE SAUCE

1 cup tomato puree or paste
½ cup water
fresh oregano, chopped
2 garlic cloves, peeled and
    crushed
1 onion, grated
1 level teaspoon sugar
freshly ground black pepper

THE TOPPINGS

olive oil
finely grated fresh parmesan
    cheese
chopped fresh herbs:
    oregano, basil, marjoram,
    thyme
minced (ground) meat,
browned in a frying pan and
    drained
sliced cabanossi
sliced button mushrooms
black olives, stoned
stuffed olives
artichoke halves
sliced hearts of palm
onion rings, cooked in a
    little oil until soft
red, green, yellow capsicum
    (pepper), sliced
anchovies
raw peeled prawns (shrimps)
smoked oysters or mussels
ham cubes
sliced salami
pineapple pieces
sun-dried tomatoes
sun-dried capsicum (pepper)

THE CHEESES

grated fresh parmesan (to
    sprinkle on the base with
    the tomato sauce)
shredded mozzarella (for the
    final topping)

BY MIXER

PLACE THE YEAST and water in a large mixer bowl. Stir to dissolve yeast. Add the remaining ingredients and almost all of the flour and mix, using the dough hook and a low speed, until the dough comes together and leaves the sides and bottom of the bowl. Knead for three minutes, adding the extra flour if necessary. Knead by hand on a lightly floured board for one minute or until the dough is no longer sticky.

BY FOOD PROCESSOR

PLACE THE YEAST and water in the food processor bowl fitted with the steel blade. Pulse for 10 seconds to mix. Add the remaining ingredients and almost all of the flour and process, with several pulses to mix, for about one minute. Add enough of the remaining flour so that the dough comes together. Knead by hand on a lightly floured board for one minute or until the dough is no longer sticky.

If you have a small food processor, process the dough in two batches and do not overwork dough.

THE NEXT STEP

PLACE THE DOUGH in a lightly oiled bowl and turn dough over so that it is very thinly coated all over with oil. Put the bowl in a large plastic bag and leave in a warm place until the dough has doubled in size.
PUNCH DOWN and knead for 10 seconds so that the dough is back to its original size. Pat, pull, roll or stretch the dough into a large rectangle and place on a shallow greased baking tray.
PLACE ALL INGREDIENTS in a small saucepan and cook over a low heat for five minutes, stirring occasionally. Cool.

PUTTING IT ALL TOGETHER

PREHEAT OVEN to hot (220°C/425°F).
BRUSH THE BASE with some extra olive oil and sprinkle on a layer of parmesan cheese.
SPREAD WITH the sauce. Top with a variety of toppings and drizzle on olive oil.
BAKE FOR 20 to 25 minutes or until the underside is browned. Sprinkle on the shredded mozzarella and return to the oven until the cheese melts. Eat immediately.

When hungry sons are too impatient to wait, I leave out the second rising of the dough. After the dough has been mixed, I ease it onto a greased tray with olive oiled fingers and leave it in a warm place while I gather together and prepare the bits and pieces for the sauce and the topping.

True Blue Dinki Di Fair Dinkum Aussie Bread

¼ cup wattle seeds

1¾ cups boiling water

20 g (¾ oz) fresh yeast or
   1 sachet dried yeast

½ level teaspoon salt

2 tablespoons golden syrup

2 tablespoons macadamia oil

½ cup cold cooked brown
   rice

2 cups wholemeal (whole-
   wheat) flour

1 cup rye flour

½ to 1 cup bread making
   flour or plain (all-purpose)
   flour sifted with 1 level
   teaspoon gluten flour

GLAZE

cold tea or a little vegemite
   mixed with cold water or
   dust with flour

Pour the boiling water over the wattle seeds and cool to lukewarm for fresh yeast and warm for dried yeast. Strain and discard half of the wattle seeds. Re-measure water and make up to 1½ cups.

BY HAND

PLACE THE YEAST in a large mixing bowl, add the wattle seeds and liquid and stir until the yeast dissolves. Add the salt, golden syrup, oil, cooked rice and the wholemeal and rye flours and beat very well with a wooden spoon. Add almost all of the remaining flour, a half a cupful at a time. When the dough becomes too stiff for the spoon, use just one floured hand to knead the dough in the bowl. TURN THE DOUGH onto a lightly floured board and knead for five minutes or until the dough no longer sticks to your hands or the board and it is smooth and elastic. Use just a very light sprinkling of flour on the board to stop the dough from sticking.

BY MIXER

PLACE THE YEAST and water in a large mixer bowl. Stir to dissolve yeast. Add the remaining ingredients and almost all of the flour and mix, using the dough hook and a low speed, until the dough comes together and leaves the sides and bottom of the bowl. Knead for three minutes, adding the extra flour if necessary. Knead by hand on a lightly floured board for one minute or until the dough is no longer sticky.

BY FOOD PROCESSOR

PLACE THE YEAST and water in the food processor bowl fitted with the steel blade. Pulse for 10 seconds to mix. Add the remaining ingredients, except the brown rice, and almost all of the flour. Process, with several pulses to mix, for about one minute. Add enough of the remaining flour so that the dough comes together. On a lightly floured board, knead in the brown rice for one minute.

If you have a small food processor, process the dough in two batches and do not overwork dough.

THE NEXT STEP

PLACE THE DOUGH in a lightly oiled bowl and turn dough over so that it is very thinly coated all over with oil. Put the bowl in a large plastic bag and leave in a warm place until the dough has doubled in size.

RIGHT: *Three Cheese Bread (page 72)*

PUNCH DOWN and knead for 10 seconds so that the dough is back to its original size. Place the dough on a greased baking tray and shape into a round. Cover with a dry cloth and leave to rise until nearly doubled in size again.

PREHEAT OVEN to moderately hot (200°C/400°F).

CUT A SHALLOW cross in the top with a very sharp knife or a single edged razor blade. Brush lightly with cold tea or vegemite and water or dust with flour. Bake for 35 to 40 minutes or until the loaf sounds hollow when tapped on the bottom and there is no stale beer smell. Cool on a wire rack. This is great served with King Island butter and Tasmanian leatherwood honey.

I did enjoy creating this totally original tribute of mine to multiculturalism. I have tried to include a bit of everything and this has made a great tasting bread. If you can think of anything else you'd like to add, add it by all means.

Pesto and Pine Nut Bread

20 g (¾ oz) fresh yeast or
  1 sachet dried yeast
1¼ cups water, lukewarm
  for fresh yeast, warm for
  dried yeast
1 level teaspoon salt
2 tablespoons pesto (see
recipe for pesto below or use
  prepared pesto from
  supermarket)
2 level tablespoons grated
  parmesan cheese
¼ cup pine nuts
2 cups wholemeal (whole-
  wheat) flour
1½ to 2 cups bread making
  flour or plain (all-purpose)
  flour sifted with 2 level
  teaspoons gluten flour

GLAZE
milk

BY HAND
PLACE THE YEAST in a large mixing bowl, add the water and stir until the yeast dissolves. Add the salt, pesto, cheese, pine nuts and wholemeal flour and beat very well with a wooden spoon. Add almost all of the remaining flour, a half a cupful at a time. When the dough becomes too stiff for the spoon, use just one floured hand to knead the dough in the bowl.

TURN THE DOUGH onto a lightly floured board and knead for five minutes or until the dough no longer sticks to your hands or the board and the dough is smooth and elastic. Use just a very light sprinkling of flour on the board to stop the dough from sticking.

BY MIXER
PLACE THE YEAST and water in a large mixer bowl. Stir to dissolve yeast. Add the remaining ingredients and almost all of the bread making flour and mix, using the dough hook and a low speed, until the dough comes together and leaves the sides and bottom of the bowl. Knead for three minutes, adding the extra flour if necessary. Knead by hand on a lightly floured board for one minute or until the dough is no longer sticky.

LEFT: *Olive and Onion Bread (page 68)*

PESTO

90 g (3 oz) basil leaves, stems and thick veins removed

2 tablespoons pine nuts, lightly roasted in a dry frying pan

2 large cloves garlic, peeled and crushed

½ cup olive oil

4 tablespoons freshly grated parmesan cheese

freshly ground black pepper

BY FOOD PROCESSOR

PLACE THE YEAST and water in the food processor bowl fitted with the steel blade. Pulse for 10 seconds to mix. Add the remaining ingredients and almost all of the bread making flour and process, with several pulses to mix, for about one minute. Add enough of the remaining flour so that the dough comes together. Knead by hand on a lightly floured board for one minute or until the dough is no longer sticky.

If you have a small food processor, process the dough in two batches and do not overwork dough.

THE NEXT STEP

PLACE THE DOUGH in a lightly oiled bowl and turn dough over so that it is thinly coated all over with oil. Put the bowl in a large plastic bag and leave in a warm place until the dough has doubled in size.

PUNCH DOWN and knead for 10 seconds so that the dough is back to its original size. Place the dough on a greased baking tray and flatten into a long oval. Using a large fresh basil leaf as a guide, form into a leaf shape. Use a thin sharp knife or a single edged razor blade to cut veins in the dough. Cover with a dry cloth and leave to rise until doubled in size again.

PREHEAT OVEN to moderate (180°C/350°F).

BRUSH LIGHTLY with a little milk and bake for 30 to 35 minutes or until the bread sounds hollow when tapped on the bottom and there is no stale beer smell. Cool on a wire rack.

SHAPING THIS BREAD is very easy. Just look at a single large basil leaf and pull, stretch and cut the dough so that it looks like it.

PLACE THE BASIL, pine nuts, garlic and half of the oil in a food processor or blender and process, in short pulses, until the mixture is finely chopped and smooth. With the processor still running, add the remaining oil very gradually in a thin stream. Transfer into a bowl and stir in the cheese and black pepper. Cover and refrigerate.

Don't overprocess the pesto as this can make it bitter. You will make more pesto than you need for the bread but having leftover real pesto stored in the refrigerator is like having money in the bank.

Tomato and Thyme Bread

20 g (¾ oz) fresh yeast or
   1 sachet dried yeast
1¼ cups water, lukewarm
   for fresh yeast, warm for
   dried yeast
½ level teaspoon salt
1 level teaspoon sugar
1 tablespoon oil
2 tablespoons tomato paste
1 tablespoon fresh thyme
   leaves or 1 teaspoon
   dried thyme leaves
2 cups wholemeal (whole-
   wheat) flour
1½ to 2 cups bread making
   flour or plain (all-purpose)
   flour sifted with 2 level
   teaspoons gluten flour

BY HAND

PLACE THE YEAST in a large mixing bowl, add the water and stir until the yeast dissolves. Add the salt, sugar, oil, tomato paste, thyme and wholemeal flour and beat very well with a wooden spoon. Add almost all of the remaining flour, a half a cupful at a time. When the dough becomes too stiff for the spoon, use just one floured hand to knead the dough in the bowl.

TURN THE DOUGH onto a lightly floured board and knead for five minutes or until the dough no longer sticks to your hands or the board and the dough is smooth and elastic. Use just a very light sprinkling of flour on the board to stop the dough from sticking.

BY MIXER

PLACE THE YEAST and water in a large mixer bowl. Stir to dissolve yeast. Add the remaining ingredients and almost all of the flour and mix, using the dough hook and a low speed, until the dough comes together and leaves the sides and bottom of the bowl. Knead for three minutes, adding the extra flour if necessary. Knead by hand on a lightly floured board for one minute or until the dough is no longer sticky.

BY FOOD PROCESSOR

PLACE THE YEAST and water in the food processor bowl fitted with the steel blade. Pulse for 10 seconds to mix. Add the remaining ingredients and almost all of the flour and process, with several pulses to mix, for about one minute. Add enough of the remaining flour so that the dough comes together. Knead by hand on a lightly floured board for one minute until the dough is no longer sticky.

If you have a small food processor, process the dough in two batches and do not overwork dough.

THE NEXT STEP

PLACE THE DOUGH in a lightly oiled bowl and turn dough over so that it is thinly coated all over with oil. Put the bowl in a large plastic bag and leave in a warm place until the dough has doubled in size.

PUNCH DOWN and knead for 10 seconds so that the dough is back to its original size. Knead in a little extra flour if necessary to make a very firm dough. Pinch off a golf ball size piece of dough and put to one side.

SHAPE THE REMAINDER of the dough into a round and cut a cross in the top. Make a shallow hole in the centre of the cross. Shape the reserved piece of dough to make a tomato stalk and base (calyx) and place in the hole. Cover with a dry cloth and leave to rise until nearly doubled in size again.

PREHEAT OVEN to moderate (180°C/350°F).

BAKE FOR 35 to 40 minutes or until the loaf sounds hollow when tapped on the bottom and there is no stale beer smell. Cool on a wire rack.

When you shape this dough, make sure it is very firm. I have ended up with breads that flattened out and so it needed a great deal of talking to convince others that it was a new species of tomato with a flat base.

Banana and Walnut Bread

20g (¾ oz) fresh yeast OR 1 sachet dried yeast

½ cup water, lukewarm for fresh yeast, warm for dried yeast

1 level teaspoon salt

2 tablespoons butter or oil

2 tablespoons light honey

2 eggs at room temperature, lightly beaten

1 cup mashed ripe bananas

1 level teaspoon ground cinnamon

½ level teaspoon ground nutmeg

2 cups wholemeal (whole wheat) flour

1½ to 2 cups breadmaking flour OR 1½ to 2 cups plain (all-purpose) flour sifted with 2 level teaspoons gluten flour

1 cup chopped walnuts

GLAZE
egg yolk and a little salt beaten together

BY HAND

PLACE THE YEAST in a large mixing bowl, add the water and stir until the yeast dissolves. Add the salt, butter, honey, eggs, mashed banana, spices and wholemeal flour and beat very well with a wooden spoon. Add almost all the remaining flour, a half a cupful at a time and when the dough becomes too stiff for the spoon, use just one floured hand to knead the dough in the bowl. Turn onto a lightly floured board and knead for five minutes or until the dough no longer sticks to your hands and the board and it is smooth and elastic. Use just a very light sprinkling of flour on the board to stop the dough from sticking.

BY MIXER

PLACE THE YEAST and wa el in a large mixer bowl. Stir to dissolve yeast. Add the remaining ingredients ex~ept the walnuts and almost all of the flour and mix, using the dough hook and a low speed, until the dough comes together and leaves the sides and bottom of the bowl. Knead for three minutes adding the extra flour if necessary.

KNEAD BY HAND on a lightly floured board for one minute until the dough is no longer sticky.

By food processor

PLACE THE YEAST and water in the food processor bowl fitted with the steel blade. Pulse for ten seconds to mix. Add the remaining ingredients except the walnuts and almost all of the flour and process with several pulses to mix for about one minute. Add enough of the remaining flour so that the dough comes together. Knead in by hand the walnuts on a lightly floured board.

If you have a small food processor, process the dough in two batches and do not overwork dough.

ALL METHODS OF MIXING

PLACE THE DOUGH in a lightly oiled bowl and turn dough over so that it is thinly coated all over with oil. Put the bowl in a large plastic bag and leave in a warm place until the dough has doubled in size. Punch down and knead for 30 seconds so that the dough is back to its original size. Divide the dough into two and flatten each piece into an oval. Spread the chopped walnuts on top. Roll up and curve the ends to make banana shapes. Place alongside each other on a lightly greased baking tray and join at one end. Cover with a dry cloth and leave to rise until doubled in size again. Use the beaten yolk to paint stripes down the length of the bananas. Bake in a preheated moderate oven for 30 to 35 minutes or until the bread sounds hollow when tapped on the bottom and there is no stale beer smell. Cool on a wire rack

This is a great way of using up those dead bananas in the fruit bowl. You can claim that's why they were there for so long too. You can use non-squashy ones but the flavour is not the same.

Pumpkin Bread

20 g (¾ oz) fresh yeast or
  1 sachet dried yeast
1 cup water, lukewarm for
  fresh yeast, warm for dried
  yeast
1 level teaspoon salt
2 tablespoons light honey
2 tablespoons oil
2 eggs at room temperature,
  lightly beaten
2 cups grated fresh pumpkin
½ cup hulled pumpkin seeds
½ level teaspoon garam
  masala or ground nutmeg
3½ to 4 cups bread making
  flour or plain (all-purpose)
  flour sifted with 2 level
  teaspoons gluten flour

GLAZE
milk

BY HAND

PLACE THE YEAST in a large mixing bowl, add the water and stir until the yeast dissolves. Add the salt, honey, oil, eggs, grated pumpkin, seeds, garam masala and flour and beat very well with a wooden spoon. Add almost all of the remaining flour, a half a cupful at a time. When the dough becomes too stiff for the spoon, use just one floured hand to knead the dough in the bowl.

TURN THE DOUGH onto a lightly floured board and knead for five minutes or until the dough no longer sticks to your hands or the board and it is smooth and elastic. Use just a very light sprinkling of flour on the board to stop the dough from sticking.

BY MIXER

PLACE THE YEAST and water in a large mixer bowl. Stir to dissolve yeast. Add the remaining ingredients and almost all of the flour and mix, using the dough hook and a low speed, until the dough comes together and leaves the sides and bottom of the bowl. Knead for three minutes, adding the extra flour if necessary. Knead by hand on a lightly floured board for one minute or until the dough is no longer sticky.

BY FOOD PROCESSOR

PLACE THE YEAST and water in the food processor bowl fitted with the steel blade. Pulse for 10 seconds to mix. Add the remaining ingredients, except the pumpkin seeds, and almost all of the flour. Process, with several pulses to mix, for about one minute. Add enough of the remaining flour so that the dough comes together. Knead in the pumpkin seeds, by hand, on a lightly floured board.

If you have a small food processor, process the dough in two batches and do not overwork dough.

THE NEXT STEP

PLACE THE DOUGH in a lightly oiled bowl and turn dough over so that it is thinly coated all over with oil. Put the bowl in a large plastic bag and leave in a warm place until the dough has doubled in size.

PUNCH DOWN and knead for 10 seconds so that the dough is back to its original size. Knead in a little extra flour if necessary to make a very firm dough. Divide the dough into two pieces and shape each piece into balls.

PUSH TWO FLOURED FINGERS into the centre of each ball and through to the base. Make shallow slashes with a very sharp thin knife or singled edged razor blade around the sides of the loaves to make pumpkin-like grooves. Place on a greased baking tray and cover with a dry cloth and leave to rise until doubled in size again.

PREHEAT OVEN to moderate (180°C/350°F).

Brush lightly with a little milk and bake for 25 to 30 minutes or until the bread sounds hollow when tapped on the bottom and there is no stale beer smell. Cool on a wire rack.

Most recipes for pumpkin bread list cooked pumpkin in the ingredients. I can never remember to cook it ahead and wait for it to cool, so I tried grating raw peeled pumpkin. And it worked, but use cooked pumpkin if you prefer.

Mushroom Bread

2 tablespoons butter or oil
1 medium onion, finely
  chopped
250 g (8 oz) fresh
  mushrooms, finely chopped
30 g (1 oz) fresh yeast or 1½
  sachets dried yeast
1 cup water, lukewarm for
  fresh yeast, warm for dried
  yeast
2 level teaspoons salt
2 tablespoons brown sugar
1 egg, lightly beaten
  freshly grated black pepper
  pinch ground nutmeg
2 cups wholemeal (whole-
  wheat) flour
1½ to 2 cups bread making
  flour or plain (all-purpose)
  flour sifted with 1 level
  teaspoon gluten flour

GLAZE
egg white beaten with a
  little water

Melt the butter in a frying pan and slow cook the onions and mushrooms until soft. Cool.

BY HAND

PLACE THE YEAST in a large mixing bowl, add the water and stir until the yeast dissolves. Add the salt, sugar, egg, black pepper, nutmeg, cooked onions and mushrooms and the wholemeal flour and beat very well with a wooden spoon. Add almost all of the remaining flour, a half a cupful at a time. When the dough becomes too stiff for the spoon, use just one floured hand to knead the dough in the bowl.

TURN THE DOUGH onto a lightly floured board and knead for five minutes or until the dough no longer sticks to your hands or the board and it is smooth and elastic. Use just a very light sprinkling of flour on the board to stop the dough from sticking.

BY MIXER

PLACE THE YEAST and water in a large mixer bowl. Stir to dissolve yeast. Add the remaining ingredients and almost all of the bread making flour and mix, using the dough hook and a low speed, until the dough comes together and leaves the sides and bottom of the bowl. Knead for three minutes, adding the extra flour if necessary. Knead by hand on a lightly floured board for one minute or until the dough is no longer sticky.

BY FOOD PROCESSOR

PLACE THE YEAST and water in the food processor bowl fitted with the steel blade. Pulse for 10 seconds to mix. Add the remaining ingredients and almost all of the bread making flour and process, with several pulses to mix, for about one minute. Add enough of the remaining flour so that the dough comes together. Knead by hand on a lightly floured board for one minute or until the dough is no longer sticky.

If you have a small food processor, process the dough in two batches and do not overwork dough.

THE NEXT STEP

PLACE THE DOUGH in a lightly oiled bowl and turn dough over so that it is very thinly coated all over with oil. Put the bowl in a large plastic bag and leave in a warm place until the dough has doubled in size.

PUNCH DOWN and knead for 10 seconds so that the dough is back to its original size. Divide the dough into 5 equal pieces.

FLATTEN AND ROLL each piece into small log shapes. Place the dough in 5 x 440 g (14 oz) well greased soup cans and only half fill the cans. Place the cans on a baking tray for easy handling. Cover with a dry cloth and place in a warm spot until the dough rises to just above the top of the can.

PREHEAT OVEN to moderately hot (200°C/400°F).

BRUSH VERY LIGHTLY with glaze and bake for 35 to 40 minutes or until the loaves sound hollow when tapped on the bottom and there is no stale beer smell. Turn out of the cans onto a wire rack to cool.

If you want to make small mushroom breads, save all your small cans and, when filled, bake them for about 15 to 20 minutes.

Spinach Bread

20 g (¾ oz) fresh yeast or 1 sachet dried yeast
½ cup water, lukewarm for fresh yeast, warm for dried yeast
2 level teaspoons salt
1 level teaspoon sugar
1 tablespoon olive oil
250 g (8 oz) frozen chopped spinach, thawed, undrained and warmed slightly
½ level teaspoon dried granulated garlic
¼ level teaspoon ground nutmeg
freshly ground black pepper
3½ to 4 cups bread making flour or plain (all-purpose) flour sifted with 3 level teaspoons gluten flour

GLAZE
milk

BY HAND

PLACE THE YEAST in a large mixing bowl, add the water and stir until the yeast dissolves. Add the salt, sugar, oil, thawed spinach, garlic, nutmeg, black pepper and half of the flour and beat very well with a wooden spoon. Add almost all of the remaining flour, a half a cupful at a time. When the dough becomes too stiff for the spoon, use just one floured hand to knead the dough in the bowl.

TURN THE DOUGH onto a lightly floured board and knead for five minutes or until the dough no longer sticks to your hands or the board and it is elastic. Use just a very light sprinkling of flour on the board to stop the dough from sticking.

BY MIXER

PLACE THE YEAST and water in a large mixer bowl. Stir to dissolve yeast. Add the remaining ingredients and almost all of the flour and mix, using the dough hook and a low speed, until the dough comes together and leaves the sides and bottom of the bowl. Knead for three minutes, adding the extra flour if necessary. Knead by hand on a lightly floured board for one minute or until the dough is no longer sticky.

BY FOOD PROCESSOR

PLACE THE YEAST and water in the food processor bowl fitted with the steel blade. Pulse for 10 seconds to mix. Add the remaining ingredients and almost all of the flour and process, with several pulses to mix, for about one minute. Add enough of the remaining flour so that the dough comes together. Knead by hand on a lightly floured board for one minute or until the dough is no longer sticky.

If you have a small food processor, process the dough in two batches and do not overwork dough.

THE NEXT STEP

PLACE THE DOUGH in a lightly oiled bowl and turn dough over so that it is very thinly coated all over with oil. Put the bowl in a large plastic bag and leave in a warm place until the dough has doubled in size.

PUNCH DOWN and knead for 10 seconds so that the dough is back to its original size. Flatten dough and shape into a spinach leaf. Use a flat wooden spoon handle to make an indentation for the centre stalk and cut thinner veins with a sharp thin knife or a single edged razor blade. Cover with a dry cloth and leave to rise until nearly doubled in size again.

PREHEAT OVEN to moderately hot (200°C/400°F).

BRUSH LIGHTLY with milk and bake for 40 to 45 minutes or until the leaf sounds hollow when tapped on the bottom and there is no stale beer smell. Cool on a wire rack.

You can use fresh spinach in this recipe if you like but I find the frozen is so convenient. If the brand you use is more watery than the one I use you may need to add more flour.

I think of the next six breads as my 'copycat breads' as they are duplications of my favourite commercial breads. It's very easy for you to create them too. Just read the ingredients listed, their quantity and order on every bread wrapper. Most of the ingredients will be familiar to you but when it says emulsifiers use egg or lecithin granules and use a little vinegar or honey as preservatives.

Traditional Ploughperson's Loaf

20 g (¾ oz) fresh yeast or
  1 sachet dried yeast
1½ cups water, lukewarm
  for fresh yeast, warm for
  dried yeast
1 level teaspoon salt
2 tablespoons melted butter
  or oil
1 teaspoon white vinegar
¼ cup soy flour
¼ cup barley flour
1 level tablespoon lecithin
  granules
1½ cups wholemeal
  (whole-wheat) flour
¾ cup kibbled (cracked)
  wheat, cooked and drained
1½ to 2 cups bread making
  flour sifted with 2 level
  teaspoons gluten flour or
  plain (all-purpose) flour
  sifted with 4 level
  teaspoons gluten flour

GLAZE
water
cooked kibbled wheat, extra

BY HAND

PLACE THE YEAST in a large mixing bowl, add the water and stir until the yeast dissolves. Add the salt, oil, vinegar, soy flour, barley flour, lecithin and wholemeal flour and beat very well with a wooden spoon. Add the cooked wheat grains and almost all of the remaining flour, a half a cupful at a time. When the dough becomes too stiff for the spoon, use just one floured hand to knead the dough in the bowl.

TURN THE DOUGH onto a lightly floured board and knead for five minutes or until the dough no longer sticks to your hands or the board and it is smooth and elastic. Use just a very light sprinkling of flour on the board to stop the dough from sticking.

BY MIXER

PLACE THE YEAST and water in a large mixer bowl. Stir to dissolve yeast. Add the remaining ingredients and almost all of the bread making flour and mix, using the dough hook and a low speed, until the dough comes together and leaves the sides and bottom of the bowl. Knead for three minutes, adding the extra flour if necessary. Knead by hand on a lightly floured board for one minute or until the dough is no longer sticky.

BY FOOD PROCESSOR

PLACE THE YEAST and water in the food processor bowl fitted with the steel blade. Pulse for 10 seconds to mix. Add remaining ingredients, except the kibbled wheat grains, and almost all the bread making flour. Process, with several pulses to mix, for about one minute. Add enough of remaining flour so that the dough comes together. Knead in the kibbled wheat grains, by hand, on a lightly floured board for one minute or until dough is no longer sticky.

If you have a small food processor, process the dough in two batches and do not overwork dough.

THE NEXT STEP

DIVIDE THE DOUGH into two pieces and shape each piece into rounds. Place on a greased baking tray, cover with a dry cloth and leave to rise until doubled in size.

PREHEAT OVEN to moderately hot (200°C/400°F).

SPRAY LIGHTLY with water and scatter on the extra kibbled wheat.

BAKE FOR 35 to 40 minutes or until the bread sounds hollow when tapped on the bottom and there is no stale beer smell. Cool on a wire rack.

THE ADDITION of the soy flour means that this bread does not need a second rising and can be shaped, allowed to rise just once, and then baked. I prefer two risings of bread as the flavour is always so much better.

Frankie's Fruit Loaf

30 g (1 oz) fresh yeast or 1½ sachets dried yeast
1½ cups water, lukewarm for fresh yeast, warm for dried yeast
1 level teaspoon salt
2 tablespoons oil
1 level teaspoon ground cinnamon
½ level teaspoon ground nutmeg
1 level teaspoon ground cardamom
¼ teaspoon ground cloves
1½ cups bread making flour sifted with ¼ cup gluten flour or plain (all-purpose) flour sifted with ½ cup gluten flour
¾ cup rye flour
¾ to 1 cup wholemeal (whole-wheat) flour
½ cup chopped dried apricots
½ cup currants
½ cup sultanas (golden raisins)
1 cup chopped dates

DECORATION
1 cup poppyseeds

BY HAND

PLACE THE YEAST in a large mixing bowl, add the water and stir until the yeast dissolves. Add the salt, oil, spices and bread making flour and beat very well with a wooden spoon. Add the rye flour and almost all of the wholemeal flour, a half a cupful at a time. When the dough becomes too stiff for the spoon, use just one floured hand to knead the dough in the bowl.

TURN THE DOUGH onto a lightly floured board and knead for five minutes or until the dough no longer sticks to your hands or the board and the dough is elastic. Use just a very light sprinkling of flour on the board to stop the dough from sticking.

BY MIXER

PLACE THE YEAST and water in a large mixer bowl. Stir to dissolve yeast. Add the salt, oil, spices, rye flour and almost all of the bread making flour. Mix, using the dough hook and a low speed, until the dough comes together and leaves the sides and bottom of the bowl. Knead for three minutes, adding the extra flour if necessary. Knead by hand on a lightly floured board for one minute or until the dough is no longer sticky.

BY FOOD PROCESSOR

PLACE THE YEAST and water in the food processor bowl fitted with the steel blade. Pulse for 10 seconds to mix. Add the salt, oil spices, rye flour and almost all of the bread making flour and process, with several pulses to mix, for about one minute. Add enough of the remaining flour so that the dough comes together.

If you have a small food processor, process the dough in two batches and do not overwork dough.

THE NEXT STEP

PLACE THE DOUGH in a lightly oiled bowl and turn dough over so that it is thinly coated on all sides with oil. Put the bowl in a large plastic bag and leave in a warm place until the dough has doubled in size.

PUNCH DOWN and knead for 10 seconds so that the dough is back to its original size. Knead in the dried fruits. Shape into a round and roll in the poppyseeds. Place on a greased baking tray and cover with a dry cloth. Leave to rise until nearly doubled in size. PREHEAT OVEN to moderate (180°C/350°F).

Bake for 35 to 40 minutes or until the bread sounds hollow when tapped on the bottom and there is no stale beer smell. Cool on a wire rack.

There's a wonderful new supermarket a long way from where I live, but I still like to travel to it nearly every week as I enjoy shopping there so much. I love this fruit loaf that I found there and I did enjoy working out how to make it more cheaply at home.

Currant Log

20 g (¾ oz) fresh yeast or
  1 sachet dried yeast
1¼ cups water, lukewarm
  for fresh yeast, warm for
  dried yeast
¼ level teaspoon salt
½ level teaspoon ground
  cinnamon
3½ to 4 cups bread making
  flour or plain (all-purpose)
  flour sifted with 3 level
  teaspoons of gluten flour
3 cups currants

GLAZE
milk

BY HAND

PLACE THE YEAST in a large mixing bowl, add the water and stir until the yeast dissolves. Add the salt, cinnamon and half of the flour and beat very well with a wooden spoon. Add the currants and almost all of the remaining flour, a half a cupful at a time. When the dough becomes too stiff for the spoon, use just one floured hand to knead the dough in the bowl.

TURN THE DOUGH onto a lightly floured board and knead for five minutes or until the dough no longer sticks to your hands or the board and the dough is smooth and elastic. Use just a very light sprinkling of flour on the board to stop the dough from sticking.

BY MIXER

PLACE THE YEAST and water in a large mixer bowl. Stir to dissolve yeast. Add remaining ingredients and almost all of the flour and mix, using the dough hook and a low speed, until the dough comes together and leaves the sides and bottom of the bowl. Knead for three minutes, adding the extra flour if necessary. Knead by hand on a lightly floured board for one minute or until the dough is no longer sticky.

BY FOOD PROCESSOR

Place the yeast and water in the food processor bowl fitted with the steel blade. Pulse for 10 seconds to mix. Add the salt, cinnamon and almost all of the flour and process, with several pulses to mix, for about one minute. Add enough of the remaining flour so that the dough comes together. Knead in the currants, by hand, on a lightly floured board.

If you have a small food processor, process the dough in two batches and do not overwork dough.

THE NEXT STEP

Place the dough in a lightly oiled bowl and turn dough over so that it is thinly coated all over with oil. Put the bowl in a large plastic bag and leave in a warm place until the dough has doubled in size. **Punch down** and knead for 10 seconds so that the dough is back to its original size.

Shape into a 25 cm (10 in) log on a well-greased baking tray, cover with a dry cloth and leave to rise until doubled in size again. Preheat oven to moderately hot (200°C/400°F).

Brush lightly with milk and bake for 30 to 35 minutes or until the log sounds hollow when tapped on the bottom and there is no stale beer smell. Cool on a wire rack and, when completely cold, store in a sealed plastic bag to keep soft.

When I first attempted to copy this bread, I didn't realise just how many currants there were in it. I started with just a cup, then another cup and finally decided three cups was just enough. It's a very slow rising dough (it's all those currants). If you want to speed it up and change its texture, add the currants after the dough has risen.

Raisin and Rice Bread

30 g (1 oz) fresh yeast or
  1½ sachets dried yeast
1½ cups water, lukewarm
  for fresh, warm for dried
1 level teaspoon salt
1 level teaspoon brown sugar
  or honey
2 tablespoons oil
1 teaspoon white vinegar
¼ cup roasted barley flour
1 level tablespoon lecithin
  granules
1 level tablespoon soy flour
½ cup cooked brown rice
½ cup raisins
1 cup bread making flour
  sifted with 1 level teaspoon
  gluten flour or plain (all-
  purpose) flour sifted with 2
  level teaspoons gluten flour
2½ to 3 cups wholemeal
  (whole-wheat) flour

In this recipe you will need to roast the barley flour, until just tinted, in a preheated moderate (180°C/350°F) oven.

BY HAND

PLACE THE YEAST in a large mixing bowl, add the water and stir until the yeast dissolves. Add the salt, sugar, oil, vinegar, barley flour, lecithin, soy flour, cooked brown rice, raisins, bread making flour, and half of the wholemeal flour and beat very well with a wooden spoon. Add almost all of the remaining flour, a half a cupful at a time. When the dough becomes too stiff for the spoon, use just one floured hand to knead the dough in the bowl.

TURN THE DOUGH onto a lightly floured board and knead for five minutes or until the dough no longer sticks to your hands or the board and it is smooth and elastic. Use just a very light sprinkling of flour on the board to stop the dough from sticking.

BY MIXER

PLACE THE YEAST and water in the food processor bowl fitted with the steel blade. Stir to dissolve yeast. Add the remaining ingredients and almost all of the wholemeal flour and mix, using the dough hook and a low speed, until the dough comes together and leaves the sides and bottom of the bowl. Knead for three minutes, adding the extra flour if necessary. Knead by hand on a lightly floured board for one minute or until the dough is no longer sticky.

BY FOOD PROCESSOR

PLACE THE YEAST and water in a large mixer bowl. Pulse for 10 seconds to mix. Add the remaining ingredients and almost all of the wholemeal flour and process, with several pulses to mix, for about one minute. Add enough of the remaining flour so that the dough comes together. Knead by hand on a lightly floured board for one minute or until the dough is no longer sticky.

If you have a small food processor, process the dough in two batches and do not overwork dough.

THE NEXT STEP

FLATTEN THE DOUGH into a 1 cm (½ in) thick oval and roll up. Pinch the ends together and place with the smooth side uppermost in a deep greased 22 x 12 cm (9 x 5 in) pan. Cover with a dry cloth and leave the dough until it rises to the top of the pan.

PREHEAT OVEN to hot (220°C/425°F).

BAKE FOR 15 minutes, then reduce the heat to moderate

(180°C/350°F). Bake for a further 20 minutes or until the bread sounds hollow when tapped on the bottom and there is no stale beer smell. Turn out of the pan and cool on a wire rack. For a soft crust cover loosely with a cloth as the bread cools.

This bread has only one rising. The lightly roasted barley flour in it has a magical effect on the dough (I'm not exactly sure why but the most informed people have assured me it is so).

Swiss Herr Doktor's Bread

2 cups boiling water
1 cup kibbled (cracked) rye grains
½ cup kibbled (cracked) wheat grains
20 g (¾ oz) fresh yeast or 1 sachet dried yeast
1 level teaspoon ground rock salt
1 level teaspoon light honey
2 tablespoons oil
1 teaspoon vinegar
2 level tablespoons soy flour
¼ cup oat bran
2 level tablespoons rice bran
1 level tablespoon soy fibre (optional)
1 cup rye flour
2 to 2½ cups bread making flour or plain (all-purpose) flour sifted with 2 level teaspoons gluten flour

Pour the boiling water over the kibbled grains to soften them. Let the water cool to lukewarm for fresh yeast and warm for dried yeast. Strain the grain and re-measure the water. Add water, if necessary, to make up to 1½ cups.

BY HAND
PLACE THE YEAST in a large mixing bowl, add the water and stir until the yeast dissolves. Add the salt, honey, oil, vinegar, soy flour, oat bran, rice bran, soy fibre, rye flour and half of the bread making flour and beat very well with a wooden spoon. Add almost all of the remaining flour, a half a cupful at a time. When the dough becomes too stiff for the spoon, use just one floured hand to knead the dough in the bowl.
TURN THE DOUGH onto a lightly floured board and knead for five minutes or until the dough no longer sticks to your hands or the board and it is smooth and elastic. Use just a very light sprinkling of flour on the board to stop the dough from sticking. Knead in the cooked grains.

BY MIXER
PLACE THE YEAST and water in a large mixer bowl. Stir to dissolve yeast. Add the remaining ingredients, except the cooked grains, and almost all of the bread making flour. Mix, using the dough hook and a low speed, until the dough comes together and leaves the sides and bottom of the bowl.
KNEAD FOR three minutes, adding the extra flour if necessary. Knead by hand on a lightly floured board for one minute or until the dough is no longer sticky. Knead in the cooked grains.

BY FOOD PROCESSOR
PLACE THE YEAST and water in the food processor bowl fitted with the steel blade. Pulse for 10 seconds to mix. Add the remaining ingredients, except the cooked grains, and almost all of the bread making flour.

PROCESS, with several pulses to mix, for about one minute. Add enough of the remaining flour so that the dough comes together. Knead by hand on a lightly floured board for one minute or until the dough is no longer sticky. Knead in the cooked grains.If you have a small food processor, process the dough in two batches and do not overwork dough.

THE NEXT STEP

FLATTEN THE DOUGH into a 1 cm (½ in) thick rectangle and roll up. Pinch the ends together and place with the smooth side uppermost in a deep greased 22 x 12 cm (9 x 5 in) pan. Cover with a dry cloth and leave the dough until it rises to the top of the pan. Preheat oven to hot (220°C/425°F).

BAKE FOR 15 minutes, then reduce the heat to moderate (180°C/350°F). Bake for a further 25 minutes or until the bread sounds hollow when tapped on the bottom and there is no stale beer smell. Turn out of the pan and cool on a wire rack.

This bread has been produced in this country for more years than I can remember. It was my very first introduction to a health bread that was not only seen to be nutritionally sound, but really tasted good with butter and honey. I still love it. The addition of the soy flour means there's only one rising needed.

RIGHT ABOVE: Focaccia (page 45); RIGHT BELOW: Baby Brioche (page 44)

Norwegian Honey and Oat Bran Loaf

2 cups boiling water
½ cup kibbled (cracked)
maize (corn) meal
½ cup kibbled (cracked)
  wheat grains
½ cup kibbled (cracked) rye
  grains
20 g (¾ oz) fresh yeast or
  1 sachet dried yeast
2 level teaspoons salt
1 tablespoon light honey
2 tablespoons oil
1 teaspoon vinegar
¼ cup non-fat skim milk
  powder
2 level tablespoons linseeds
2 level tablespoons sesame
  seeds
2 tablespoons barley flakes
  (optional)
3½ to 4 cups bread making
  flour or plain (all-purpose)
  flour sifted with 4 level
  teaspoons gluten flour

Pour the boiling water over the kibbled grains in a saucepan and cook until grains are soft. Let the water cool, lukewarm for fresh yeast and warm for dried yeast. Strain the grain and re-measure the water. Add water, if necessary, to make up to 1¼ cups.

BY HAND

PLACE THE YEAST in a large mixing bowl, add the water and stir until the yeast dissolves. Add the salt, honey, oil, vinegar, skim milk powder, linseeds, sesame seeds, barley flakes and half of the flour and beat very well with a wooden spoon. Add the remaining flour, a half a cupful at a time and beat for five minutes. Mix in the soaked grains.

BY MIER

PLACE THE YEAST and water in a large mixer bowl. Stir to dissolve yeast. Add the remaining ingredients and almost all of the flour and mix, using the dough hook and a low speed for three minutes.

BY FOOD PROCESSOR

PLACE THE YEAST and water in the food processor bowl fitted with the steel blade. Pulse for 10 seconds to mix. Add the remaining ingredients and the flour and process, with several pulses to mix, for about one minute.

If you have a small food processor, process the dough in two batches and do not overwork dough.

THE NEXT STEP

PLACE THE BOWL in a large plastic bag and leave to rise until doubled in size. Stir with a wooden spoon until the dough is back to its original size and scrape and pour into a deep greased 22 x 12 cm (9 x 5 in) pan. Smooth the surface of the dough with oiled fingers. Cover with a dry cloth and leave the dough until it rises to the top of the pan. PREHEAT OVEN to hot (220°C/425°F).

BAKE FOR 15 minutes, then reduce the heat to moderate (180°C/350°F). Bake for a further 25 minutes or until a skewer inserted in the centre comes out clean and there is no stale beer smell. Leave in the pan for five minutes before turning out of the pan to cool on a wire rack.

This Scandinavian style loaf can't, by food law regulations, be called a bread at all. There is not enough flour in it. It's really a batter bread and is beaten not kneaded. Don't attempt to knead it on a board unless you want to have a disastrous experience you'll never forget.

LEFT: White True Sourdough Bread (page 78)

Sunflower Seed and Barley Corn Bread

½ cup kibbled (cracked) rye
  grains
½ cup kibbled (cracked)
  corn
1¾ cups boiling water
20 g (¾ oz) fresh yeast or
  1 sachet dried yeast
1 level teaspoon salt
½ cup skim milk powder
½ cup barley, cooked
½ cup sunflower seeds
2 cups wholemeal flour
1½ to 2 cups bread making
  flour or plain (all-purpose)
  flour sifted with 2 level
  teaspoons gluten flour

GLAZE
water
extra sunflower seeds

Place the kibbled rye and corn in a bowl and pour on the boiling water. Leave to cool to lukewarm for fresh yeast and warm for dried. Re-measure water and add extra if necessary to make 1½ cups.

BY HAND

PLACE THE WATER and the soaked grains in a large mixing bowl, add the yeast and stir until the yeast dissolves.

Add the salt, skim milk powder, cooked barley, sunflower seeds and the wholemeal flour. Beat very well with a wooden spoon. Add almost all of the bread making flour, a half a cupful at a time. When the dough becomes too stiff for the spoon, use just one floured hand to knead the dough in the bowl.

TURN THE DOUGH onto a lightly floured board and knead for five minutes or until the dough no longer sticks to your hands or the board and the dough is smooth and elastic. Use just a very light sprinkling of flour on the board to stop the dough from sticking.

BY MIXER

PLACE THE YEAST and water in a large mixer bowl. Stir to dissolve yeast. Add the remaining ingredients and almost all of the flour and mix, using the dough hook and a low speed, until the dough comes together and leaves the sides and bottom of the bowl. Knead for three minutes, adding the extra flour if necessary. Knead by hand on a lightly floured board for one minute or until the dough is no longer sticky.

BY FOOD PROCESSOR

PLACE THE YEAST and water in the food processor bowl fitted with the steel blade. Pulse for 10 seconds to mix. Add the remaining ingredients, except cooked barley and sunflower seeds, and almost all of the flour. Process, with several pulses to mix, for about one minute. Add enough of the remaining flour so that the dough comes together. Knead in, by hand, the cooked barley and sun-flower seeds on a lightly floured board.

If you have a small food processor, process the dough in two batches and do not overwork dough.

THE NEXT STEP

PLACE THE DOUGH in a lightly oiled bowl and turn dough over so that it is thinly coated on all sides with oil. Put the bowl in a large plastic bag and leave in a warm place until the dough has doubled in size.

PUNCH DOWN and knead for 10 seconds so that the dough is back to its original size. Shape into a round, spray lightly with water and scatter on the extra sunflower seeds. Place on a greased baking tray and cover with a dry cloth. Leave to rise until nearly doubled in size. **PREHEAT OVEN** to moderate (180°C/350°F).

BAKE FOR 35 to 40 minutes or until the bread sounds hollow when tapped on the bottom and there is no stale beer smell. Cool on a wire rack.

If you don't want to buy barley for this bread use cooked brown rice instead and no one will ever know the difference, except you.

Walnut Bread

20 g (¾ oz) fresh yeast or one sachet dried yeast

1½ cups water, lukewarm for fresh yeast, warm for dried yeast

1 level teaspoon salt

2 tablespoons light honey

¼ cup walnut oil

¼ level teaspoon ground nutmeg

2 cups wholemeal (whole-wheat) flour

1½ to 2 cups bread making flour or plain (all-purpose) flour sifted with 2 teaspoons gluten flour

½ cup walnut pieces, coarsely chopped

BY HAND

PLACE THE YEAST in a large mixing bowl, add the water and stir until the yeast dissolves. Add the salt, honey, walnut oil, nutmeg and the wholemeal flour and beat very well with a wooden spoon. Add almost all of the bread making flour, a half a cupful at a time. When the dough becomes too stiff for the spoon, use just one floured hand to knead the dough in the bowl.

TURN THE DOUGH onto a lightly floured board and knead for five minutes or until the dough no longer sticks to your hands or the board and it is smooth and elastic. Use just a very light sprinkling of flour on the board to stop the dough from sticking.

BY MIXER

PLACE THE YEAST and water in a large mixer bowl. Stir to dissolve yeast. Add the salt, honey, walnut oil, nutmeg, wholemeal flour and almost all of the bread making flour. Mix, using the dough hook and a low speed, until the dough comes together and leaves the sides and bottom of the bowl. Knead for three minutes, adding the extra flour if necessary. Knead by hand on a lightly floured board for one minute or until the dough is no longer sticky.

BY FOOD PROCESSOR

PLACE THE YEAST and water in the food processor bowl fitted with the steel blade. Pulse for 10 seconds to mix. Add the remaining ingredients, except for the walnuts, and almost all of the bread making flour. Process, with several pulses to mix, for about one minute. Add enough of the remaining flour so that the dough comes together. Knead by hand on a lightly floured board for one minute or until the dough is no longer sticky.

If you have a small food processor, process the dough in two batches and do not overwork dough.

THE NEXT STEP

PLACE THE DOUGH in a lightly oiled bowl and turn dough over so that it is very thinly coated all over with oil. Put the bowl in a large plastic bag and leave in a warm place until the dough has doubled in size.

ADD THE WALNUTS and punch down and knead for 10 seconds so the dough is back to its original size. Shape into a round and place on a greased baking tray. Cover with a dry cloth and leave to rise until doubled in size again.

PREHEAT OVEN to moderately hot (200°C/400°F).

Bake for 35 to 40 minutes or until the loaf sounds hollow when tapped on the bottom and there is no stale beer smell. Cool on a wire rack.

Always use the best walnuts (or even the best pecans) for this bread. Baking walnuts may be a lot cheaper but they are often very bitter. Be sure to keep your very expensive walnut oil refrigerated after opening and it will keep for ages.

Olive and Onion Bread

2 tablespoons olive oil
2 medium onions, sliced
20 g (¾ oz) fresh yeast or 1 sachet dried yeast
1½ cups water, lukewarm for fresh yeast, warm for dried yeast
½ level teaspoon salt
1 level teaspoon brown sugar
1 cup black olives, stoned
2 cups wholemeal (whole-wheat) flour
1½ to 2 cups bread making flour or plain (all-purpose) flour sifted with 2 level teaspoon gluten flour

Heat the oil in a frying pan and slowly cook the onions until soft and golden. Cool.

BY HAND

PLACE THE YEAST in a large mixing bowl, add the water and stir until the yeast dissolves. Add the salt, sugar, cooked onion, stoned olives and the wholemeal flour and beat very well with a wooden spoon. Add almost all of the bread making flour, a half a cupful at a time. When the dough becomes too stiff for the spoon, use just one floured hand to knead the dough in the bowl.

TURN THE DOUGH onto a lightly floured board and knead for five minutes or until the dough no longer sticks to your hands or the board and it is smooth and elastic. Use just a very light sprinkling of flour on the board to stop the dough from sticking.

BY MIXER

PLACE THE YEAST and water in a large mixer bowl. Stir to dissolve yeast. Add the remaining ingredients and almost all of the bread making flour and mix, using the dough hook and a low speed, until the dough comes together and leaves the sides and bottom of the bowl. Knead for three minutes, adding the extra flour if necessary. Knead by hand on a lightly floured board for one minute or until the dough is no longer sticky.

BY FOOD PROCESSOR

PLACE THE YEAST and water in the food processor bowl fitted with the steel blade. Pulse for 10 seconds to mix. Add the salt, sugar and wholemeal flour and almost all of the bread making flour and process, with several pulses to mix, for about one minute. Add enough of the remaining flour so that the dough comes together. Knead in the cooked onions and olives, by hand, on a lightly floured board.

If you have a small food processor, process the dough in two batches and do not overwork dough.

THE NEXT STEP

PLACE THE DOUGH in a lightly oiled bowl and turn dough over so that it is thinly coated all over with oil. Put the bowl in a large plastic bag and leave in a warm place until the dough has doubled in size. PUNCH DOWN and knead for 10 seconds so that the dough is back to its original size. Divide the dough into two rounds and place on a greased baking tray. Use a thin sharp knife or a single edged razor blade to cut slashes in the dough. Cover with a dry cloth and leave to rise until doubled in size again.

PREHEAT OVEN to moderately hot (200°C/400°F).

Bake for 30 to 35 minutes or until the bread sounds hollow when tapped on the bottom and there is no stale beer smell. Cool on a wire rack.

I always put the very best and fattest of black olives in this bread. I have a wonderful gadget in my collection of kitchen junk that removes the stones in a remarkably clever way, but a small sharp knife will work as well. If your olives are very, very salty, reduce the half teaspoon of salt to a pinch.

Lemon and Egg Plait

30 g (1 oz) fresh yeast or
  1½ sachets dried yeast
½ cup water, lukewarm for
  fresh yeast, warm for dried
  yeast
½ cup milk, lukewarm for
  fresh yeast, warm for dried
  yeast
2 level teaspoons salt
½ cup light honey
3 tablespoons melted butter
  or oil
juice and finely grated rind
  of 1 lemon
2 eggs, at room temperature,
  lightly beaten
2 cups wholemeal (whole-
  wheat) flour
1½ to 2 cups bread making
  flour or plain (all-purpose)
  flour sifted with 1 level
  teaspoon gluten flour

GLAZE AND DECORATION
water
sesame seeds

BY HAND

PLACE THE YEAST in a large mixing bowl, add the water and stir until the yeast dissolves. Add the milk, salt, honey, butter, lemon juice and rind, eggs and the wholemeal flour and beat very well with a wooden spoon. Add almost all of the bread making flour, a half a cupful at a time. When the dough becomes too stiff for the spoon, use just one floured hand to knead the dough in the bowl. TURN THE DOUGH onto a lightly floured board and knead for five minutes or until the dough no longer sticks to your hands or the board and it is smooth and elastic. Use just a very light sprinkling of flour on the board to stop the dough from sticking.

BY MIXER

PLACE THE YEAST and water in a large mixer bowl. Stir to dissolve yeast. Add the remaining ingredients and almost all of the bread making flour and mix, using the dough hook and a low speed, until the dough comes together and leaves the sides and bottom of the bowl. Knead for three minutes, adding the extra flour if necessary. Knead by hand on a lightly floured board for one minute or until the dough is no longer sticky.

BY FOOD PROCESSOR

PLACE THE YEAST and water in the food processor bowl fitted with the steel blade. Pulse for 10 seconds to mix. Add the remaining ingredients and almost all of the bread making flour and process, with several pulses to mix, for about one minute. Add enough of the remaining flour so that the dough comes together. Knead by hand on a lightly floured board for one minute or until the dough is no longer sticky.

If you have a small food processor, process the dough in two batches and do not overwork dough.

THE NEXT STEP

PLACE THE DOUGH in a lightly oiled bowl and turn dough over so that it is very thinly coated all over with oil. Put the bowl in a large plastic bag and leave in a warm place until the dough has doubled in size.

PUNCH DOWN and knead for 10 seconds so the dough is back to its original size. Divide the dough into 3 pieces. Stretch, shape and roll each piece into a long rope. Place the ropes of dough on a greased baking tray and plait (braid). Cover with a dry cloth and leave to rise until nearly doubled in size.

PREHEAT OVEN to moderate (180°C/350°F).

SPRAY LIGHTLY with water and sprinkle on the sesame seeds. Bake for 35 to 40 minutes or until the plait sounds hollow when tapped on the bottom and there is no stale beer smell. Cool on a wire rack.

As with all bread plaits (or braids as our American cousins say), try to do more than three strands. If even three is too hard for you, shape the dough into a long rope, double it and then twist it.

Use light coloured and mild flavoured honey in bread recipes. Very dark strong tasting honeys can dominate too much and, as well, they can mysteriously affect the rise of some doughs, or so I have been told.

Apricot Bread

20 g (¾ oz) fresh yeast or
  1 sachet dried yeast
¼ cup water, lukewarm for
  fresh yeast, warm for dried
  yeast
¾ cup canned apricot
  nectar (juice) at room
  temperature
1 level teaspoon salt
1 tablespoon melted butter
  or oil
1 egg, lightly beaten
2 cups wholemeal (whole-
  wheat) flour
1½ cups bread making flour
  or plain (all-purpose) flour
  sifted with 1 level teaspoon
  gluten flour
½ cup chopped dried
  apricots
½ cup chopped macadamia
  nuts

BY HAND

PLACE THE YEAST in a large mixing bowl, add the water and stir until the yeast dissolves. Add the apricot nectar, salt, butter, egg and the wholemeal flour and beat very well with a wooden spoon. Add almost all of the remaining flour, a half a cupful at a time. When the dough becomes too stiff for the spoon, use just one floured hand to knead the dough in the bowl.

TURN THE DOUGH onto a lightly floured board and knead for five minutes or until the dough no longer sticks to your hands or the board and it is smooth and elastic. Use just a very light sprinkling of flour on the board to stop the dough from sticking.

BY MIXER

PLACE THE YEAST and water in a large mixer bowl. Stir to dissolve yeast. Add the remaining ingredients, except the apricots and nuts, and almost all of the bread making flour. Mix, using the dough hook and a low speed, until the dough comes together and leaves the sides and bottom of the bowl. Knead for three minutes, adding the extra flour if necessary. Knead by hand on a lightly floured board for one minute or until the dough is no longer sticky.

BY FOOD PROCESSOR

PLACE THE YEAST and water in the food processor bowl fitted with the steel blade. Pulse for 10 seconds to mix. Add the remaining ingredients, except the apricots and nuts, and almost all of the bread making flour. Process, with several pulses to mix, for about one minute. Add enough of the remaining flour so that the dough comes together. Knead by hand on a lightly floured board for one minute or until the dough is no longer sticky.

If you have a small food processor, process the dough in two batches and do not overwork dough.

THE NEXT STEP

PLACE THE DOUGH in a lightly oiled bowl and turn dough over so that it is very thinly coated all over with oil. Put the bowl in a large plastic bag and leave in a warm place until the dough has doubled in size.

PUNCH DOWN and knead for 10 seconds so that the dough is back to its original size. Flatten the dough into a large oval and spread on the apricots and nuts. Roll up into a long shape and place on a greased baking tray. Snip the top at a 45° angle with scissors or a sharp thin knife. Cover with a dry cloth and leave to rise until nearly doubled in size again.

PREHEAT OVEN to moderate (180°C/350°F).

BAKE FOR 40 to 45 minutes or until the bread sounds hollow when tapped on the bottom and there is no stale beer smell. Cool on a wire rack.

There is no sugar in this recipe as the apricot nectar or juice is sweet enough. You can use nuts other than the expensive macadamias (they were 'Queensland nuts' to me as a child) but I love the buttery crunchiness of them.

Three Cheese Bread

20 g (¾ oz) fresh yeast or
1 sachet dried yeast
½ cup water, lukewarm for
fresh yeast, warm for dried
1 cup milk, lukewarm for fresh
yeast, warm for dried yeast
1 level teaspoon salt
1 level teaspoon sugar
1 tablespoon oil or melted
butter
2 cups wholemeal (whole-
wheat) flour
1½ to 2 cups bread making
flour or plain (all-purpose)
flour sifted with 1 level
teaspoon gluten flour
½ cup finely grated strong
cheddar cheese
¼ cup grated parmesan
1 cup of small cubes of
fetta cheese

BY HAND

PLACE THE YEAST in a large mixing bowl, add the water and stir until the yeast dissolves. Add the milk, salt, sugar, oil and the wholemeal flour and beat very well with a wooden spoon. Add almost all of the bread making flour, a half a cupful at a time. When the dough becomes too stiff for the spoon, use just one floured hand to knead the dough in the bowl.

TURN THE DOUGH onto a lightly floured board and knead for five minutes or until the dough no longer sticks to your hands or the board and it is smooth and elastic. Use just a very light sprinkling of flour on the board to stop the dough from sticking.

BY MIXER

PLACE THE YEAST and water in a large mixer bowl. Stir to dissolve yeast. Add the remaining ingredients, except the cheeses, and almost all of the bread making flour. Mix, using the dough hook and a low speed, until the dough comes together and leaves the sides and bottom of the bowl. Knead for three minutes, adding the extra flour if necessary. Knead by hand on a lightly floured board for one minute or until the dough is no longer sticky.

GLAZE AND DECORATION
water
poppyseeds

BY FOOD PROCESSOR

PLACE THE YEAST and water in the food processor bowl fitted with the steel blade. Pulse for 10 seconds to mix. Add the remaining ingredients, except the cheeses, and almost all of the flour. Process, with several pulses to mix, for about one minute. Add enough of the bread making flour so that the dough comes together. Knead by hand on a lightly floured board for one minute or until the dough is no longer sticky.

If you have a small food processor, process the dough in two batches and do not overwork dough.

THE NEXT STEP

PLACE THE DOUGH in a lightly oiled bowl and turn dough over so that it is very thinly coated all over with oil. Put the bowl in a large plastic bag and leave in a warm place until the dough has doubled in size.

PUNCH DOWN and knead for 10 seconds so that the dough is back to its original size. Flatten the dough into a large oval and spread on all of the cheeses. Roll up tightly into a log shape.

Cut off a piece about the size of a tennis ball and cut off one-third of the remaining dough. Shape all three pieces of dough into rounds and place the largest on a greased baking tray. Place the second largest one on top.

FLOUR TWO FINGERS and push down through the top dough ball into the large one. Repeat with the smallest ball of dough. Dust with flour. Cover with a dry cloth and leave to rise until nearly doubled in size again.

PREHEAT OVEN to moderately hot (200°C/400°F).

BAKE FOR 35 to 40 minutes or until the bread sounds hollow when tapped on the bottom and there is no stale beer smell. Cool on a wire rack.

This doesn't have to be a three cheese bread. It could be a two cheese, four cheese, five cheese or even just a one cheese bread. However, the cheeses used are the cheeses most likely to be found in my refrigerator.

Green Herb and Garlic Bread

20 g (¾ oz) fresh yeast or
 1 sachet dried yeast
1½ cups water, lukewarm
 for fresh yeast, warm for
 dried yeast
2 level teaspoons salt
1 level teaspoon sugar
2 tablespoons olive oil
1 to 2 tablespoons finely
 chopped fresh parsley
1 teaspoon finely chopped
 fresh rosemary
¼ level teaspoon dried
 granulated garlic
freshly ground black pepper
1 cup rye flour
2 cups wholemeal (whole-
 wheat) flour
½ to 1 cup bread making
 flour or plain (all-purpose)
 flour sifted with 1 level
 teaspoon gluten flour

BY HAND

PLACE THE YEAST in a large mixing bowl, add the water and stir until the yeast dissolves. Add the salt, sugar, oil, herbs, garlic, black pepper, rye and wholemeal flours and beat very well with a wooden spoon. Add almost all of the bread making flour, a half a cupful at a time. When the dough becomes too stiff for the spoon, use just one floured hand to knead the dough in the bowl.

TURN THE DOUGH onto a lightly floured board and knead for five minutes or until the dough no longer sticks to your hands or the board and it is smooth and elastic. Use just a very light sprinkling of flour on the board to stop the dough from sticking.

BY MIXER

PLACE THE YEAST and water in a large mixer bowl. Stir to dissolve yeast. Add the remaining ingredients and almost all of the bread making flour and mix, using the dough hook and a low speed, until the dough comes together and leaves the sides and bottom of the bowl. Knead for three minutes, adding the extra flour if necessary. Knead by hand on a lightly floured board for one minute or until the dough is no longer sticky.

BY FOOD PROCESSOR

PLACE THE YEAST and water in the food processor bowl fitted with the steel blade. Pulse for 10 seconds to mix. Add the remaining ingredients and almost all of the bread making flour and process, with several pulses to mix, for about one minute. Add enough of the remaining flour so that the dough comes together. Knead by hand on a lightly floured board for one minute or until the dough is no longer sticky.

   If you have a small food processor, process the dough in two batches and do not overwork dough.

THE NEXT STEP

PLACE THE DOUGH in a lightly oiled bowl and turn dough over so that it is very thinly coated all over with oil. Put the bowl in a large plastic bag and leave in a warm place until the dough has doubled in size.

PUNCH DOWN and knead for 10 seconds so that the dough is back to its original size. Shape into a round and place on a greased baking tray. Make a horseshoe shaped slash in the top of the dough with a very sharp thin knife or a single edged razor blade. Cover with a dry cloth and leave to rise until nearly doubled in size again.

PREHEAT OVEN to moderately hot (200°C/400°F).

BAKE FOR 35 to 40 minutes or until the bread sounds hollow when tapped on the bottom. Cool on a wire rack.

Don't use fresh garlic in bread doughs as the dough reacts in a very weird way and won't work as well. After washing the herbs, dry them very thoroughly, otherwise you'll end up with a wet mess on your chopping board. If you only have dried herbs, divide the fresh quantities by three.

Champion Bread

20 g (¾ oz) fresh yeast or 1 sachet dried yeast
1½ cups water, lukewarm for fresh yeast, warm for dried
2 level teaspoons salt
1 level tablespoon brown sugar
1 tablespoon oil or melted butter
1 level tablespoon gluten flour
1 level tablespoon soy flour
½ cup millet flour
3 to 3½ cups wholemeal (whole-wheat) flour

GLAZE
water
sesame seeds

BY HAND

PLACE THE YEAST in a large mixing bowl, add the water and stir until the yeast dissolves. Add the salt, sugar, oil, gluten, soy and millet flours and half of the wholemeal flour and beat very well with a wooden spoon. Add almost all of the remaining flour, a half a cupful at a time. When the dough becomes too stiff for the spoon, use just one floured hand to knead the dough in the bowl.

TURN THE DOUGH onto a lightly floured board and knead for five minutes or until the dough no longer sticks to your hands or the board and it is smooth and elastic. Use just a very light sprinkling of flour on the board to stop the dough from sticking.

BY MIXER

PLACE THE YEAST and water in a large mixer bowl. Stir to dissolve yeast. Add the remaining ingredients and almost all of the wholemeal flour and mix, using the dough hook and a low speed, until the dough comes together and leaves the sides and bottom of the bowl. Knead for three minutes, adding the extra flour if necessary. Knead by hand on a lightly floured board for one minute or until the dough is no longer sticky.

BY FOOD PROCESSOR

PLACE THE YEAST and water in the food processor bowl fitted with the steel blade. Pulse for 10 seconds to mix. Add the remaining ingredients and almost all of the wholemeal flour and process, with several pulses to mix, for about one minute. Add enough of the remaining flour so that the dough comes together. Knead by hand on a lightly floured board for one minute or until the dough is no longer sticky.

If you have a small food processor, process the dough in two batches and do not overwork dough.

THE NEXT STEP

SHAPE INTO a round, spray lightly with water and sprinkle lavishly with sesame seeds. Cover with a dry cloth and leave to rise until doubled in size.

PREHEAT OVEN to moderately hot (200°C/400°F).

Bake for 30 to 35 minutes or until the bread sounds hollow when tapped on the bottom and there is no stale beer smell. Cool on a wire rack.

This was the bread that a swimming champion of the fifties used to eat. His mother would make it and he'd go out and break swimming records. The protein rich soy flour in it means there's no need to let it rise twice.

Sourdoughs

You really need to plan ahead if you want to make sourdough breads. There is no short cut way for you to be eating sourdough breads on the same day as you start making them. There are no quick results like you get from most of the breads in this book.

Breads made from a sourdough starter base take much longer to make than breads made from commercial yeast. However, it is worth the time and effort to get to eat the wonderfully distinctive and tangy bread you make from sourdough starters.

SOURDOUGH STARTERS

There are many ways of making the sourdough starter bases for sourdough breads. When I heard of it, I really loved the idea of trapping the wild yeasts that float through the air and using them to make bread but, at first, I had no success in the chase.

I may have been just too impatient as I didn't really want to wait the two or so days it can take to snare the wild yeast beasts, in the flour and liquid trap, and then wait for another three to five days for them to really get going. I tried several times with varying results.

The starters using milk as the liquid managed to grow some pretty coloured moulds on top; with tap water there was no bubbling at all after five days and it smelt bad. It was then that I found a recipe using filtered or bottled water and just flour. I decided to give very small game hunting one more chance and it worked extremely well.

RIGHT: Blueberry Bagels (page 96)

Sourdough Wild Yeast Starter

2 cups bottled or filtered water
2 cups plain (all-purpose) flour

BLEND THE WATER and flour together in a very large glass preserving bottle fitted with a lid. Do not worry about the lumps. Lift up the lid, cover with a cloth (to keep the dust and insects out) and leave in a warmish place (not in the sun) for at least two days or until the mixture has begun to make bubbles and has taken on a spongy look.

Don't worry if the liquid separates out on top, just stir it back in. When you have succeeded in the chase, refrigerate your capture in its large glass bottle with the lid up, but covered with foil or plastic wrap. If you leave the jar closed and you have a really lively yeast, there is a remote possibility that the bottle just may explode. Very unlikely, but you never know.

Most recipes for sourdough need a cup of starter. You'll need to feed the starter the day before you bake so you don't use it all in the first loaf you make. Feeding is simple; just blend in another cup of flour and another cup of liquid. Then, leave the starter out of the refrigerator, loosely covered, for a few hours and, when it looks spongy, refrigerate again. Each time you use a cup of starter in a recipe, repeat the feeding procedure.

Speedy Sourdough Starter

15 g (½ oz) fresh yeast or 1 sachet dried yeast
1 tablespoon light honey (dark honey may not work)
2 cups water, lukewarm for fresh yeast, warm for dried
2 cups plain (all-purpose) flour

If all of the above is too much trouble, use fresh or dried yeast in your sourdough starter. It may not be as sporting but it does work every time and it is much faster.

BLEND ALL INGREDIENTS together in a very large glass preserving bottle fitted with a lid. Do not worry about the lumps. Lift up the lid, loosely cover with foil or plastic film and leave at room temperature, stirring occasionally, for a day or until bubbly and frothy. Store in the refrigerator.

Sourdoughs need food and water to stay alive. Every week, halve the sourdough starter, give one half away to a friend or an enemy and feed your half with one cup of water and one cup of flour blended together.

When you have become a real expert at sourdoughs you can finetune the taste by adding a pinch of bicarbonate of soda (baking soda) if it is too acidic, or leaving it out of the refrigerator to make a more decidedly sour taste or always keeping it refrigerated for more delicate tasting bread.

LEFT: Croissants (page 93)

White True Sourdough Bread

1 cup sourdough starter (see
   recipe page 76)
1 cup lukewarm water
2 cups bread making flour or
   plain (all-purpose) flour
   sifted with 2 level
   teaspoons gluten flour
2 level teaspoons salt
1 level teaspoon sugar
1½ to 2 cups extra bread
   making flour or plain (all-
   purpose) flour sifted with 2
   level teaspoons gluten flour
   extra flour for dusting

Place the sourdough starter and water in a bowl and stir in the flour. Blend until smooth. Place the bowl in a large plastic bag and leave overnight. If it is the middle of summer, and very hot, find the coolest part of the house but do not refrigerate.

BY HAND

THE NEXT MORNING, stir in the salt, sugar and almost all of the extra bread making flour, a half a cupful at a time. When the dough becomes too stiff for the spoon, use just one floured hand to knead the dough in the bowl.

TURN THE DOUGH onto a lightly floured board and knead for five minutes or until the dough no longer sticks to your hands or the board and it is smooth and elastic. Use just a very light sprinkling of flour on the board to stop the dough from sticking.

BY MIXER

THE NEXT MORNING, add the salt, sugar and almost all of the extra bread making flour and mix, using the dough hook and a low speed, until the dough comes together and leaves the sides and bottom of the bowl. Knead for three minutes, adding the extra flour if necessary. Knead by hand on a lightly floured board for one minute or until the dough is no longer sticky.

BY FOOD PROCESSOR

THE NEXT MORNING place the dough in the food processor bowl fitted with the steel blade. Pulse for 10 seconds. Add the remaining ingredients and almost all of the extra bread making flour and process, with several pulses to mix, for about one minute. Add enough of the remaining flour so that the dough comes together. Knead by hand on a lightly floured board for one minute or until the dough is no longer sticky.

If you have a small food processor, process the dough in two batches and do not overwork dough.

THE NEXT STEP

PLACE THE DOUGH in a lightly oiled bowl and turn the dough over so that it is very thinly coated all over with oil. Put the bowl in a large plastic bag and leave to rise in a warm place until the dough has doubled in size; about two to three hours.

PUNCH DOWN and knead the dough for 30 seconds so that the dough is back to its original size. Divide the dough into two, shape into rounds and place on a greased baking tray. Cover with a dry cloth and leave to rise in a warm place until doubled in size again; about one to two hours.

PREHEAT OVEN to moderately hot (200°C/400°F).

MAKE SHALLOW slashes with a very thin knife or a single edged razor blade. Bake for 25 to 30 minutes or until the bread sounds hollow when tapped on the bottom and there is no stale beer smell. Cool on a wire rack.

Wholemeal True Sourdough Bread

1 cup sourdough starter (see recipe page 76)
1 cup lukewarm water
2 cups bread making flour or plain (all-purpose) flour sifted with 2 level teaspoons gluten flour
2 level teaspoons salt
1 level teaspoon sugar
1½ to 2 cups wholemeal (whole-wheat) flour extra flour for dusting

Place the sourdough starter and water in a bowl and stir in the bread making flour. Blend until smooth. Place the bowl in a large plastic bag and leave overnight. If it is the middle of summer, and very hot, find the coolest part of the house but do not refrigerate.

BY HAND

THE NEXT MORNING, add the salt, sugar and almost all the wholemeal flour, a half a cupful at a time. When the dough becomes too stiff for the spoon, use just one floured hand to knead the dough in the bowl.

TURN THE DOUGH onto a lightly floured board and knead for five minutes or until the dough no longer sticks to your hands or the board and it is smooth and elastic. Use just a very light sprinkling of flour on the board to stop the dough from sticking.

BY MIXER

THE NEXT MORNING, add the remaining ingredients and almost all of the wholemeal flour and mix, using the dough hook and a low speed, until the dough comes together and leaves the sides and bottom of the bowl. Knead for three minutes, adding the extra flour if necessary. Knead by hand on a lightly floured board for one minute or until the dough is no longer sticky.

BY FOOD PROCESSOR

THE NEXT MORNING, place in the food processor bowl fitted with the steel blade. Pulse for 10 seconds. Add the remaining ingredients and almost all of the wholemeal flour and process, with several pulses to mix, for about one minute. Add enough of the remaining flour so that the dough comes together. Knead by hand on a lightly floured board for one minute or until the dough is no longer sticky.

If you have a small food processor, process the dough in two batches and do not overwork dough.

THE NEXT STEP
PLACE THE DOUGH in a lightly oiled bowl and turn the dough over so that it is very thinly coated all over with oil. Put the bowl in a large plastic bag and leave to rise in a warm place until the dough has doubled in size; about two to three hours.
PUNCH DOWN and knead the dough for 10 seconds so that the dough is back to its original size. Shape into a round and place on a greased baking tray. Dust thickly with flour, cover with a dry cloth and leave to rise in a warm place until doubled in size again; about one to two hours.
PREHEAT OVEN to moderately hot (200°C/400°F).
BAKE FOR 35 to 40 minutes or until the bread sounds hollow when tapped on the bottom and there is no stale beer smell. Cool on a wire rack.

Rye True Sourdough Bread

1 cup sourdough starter
(see recipe page 76
1 cup lukewarm water
2 cups bread making flour or
plain (all-purpose) flour
sifted with 2 level
teaspoons gluten flour
2 level teaspoons salt
1 level tablespoon brown
sugar
2 tablespoons oil or melted
butter
½ to 1 level teaspoon
caraway seeds
1½ to 2 cups rye flour

GLAZE
cold black coffee

Place the sourdough starter and water in a bowl and stir in the flour. Blend until smooth. Place the bowl in a large plastic bag and leave overnight. If it is the middle of summer, and very hot, find the coolest part of the house but do not refrigerate.

BY HAND
THE NEXT MORNING, place the sourdough mix in a large mixing bowl, add the water, salt, sugar, oil, caraway seeds and almost all of the rye flour and beat very well with a wooden spoon. When the dough becomes too stiff for the spoon, use just one floured hand to knead the dough in the bowl.
TURN THE DOUGH onto a lightly floured board and knead for five minutes or until the dough no longer sticks to your hands or the board and the dough is smooth and elastic. Use just a very light sprinkling of flour on the board to stop the dough from sticking.

BY MIXER
THE NEXT MORNING, place the sourdough mix in a large mixer bowl. Add the remaining ingredients and almost all of the rye flour and mix, using the dough hook and a low speed, until the dough comes together and leaves the sides and bottom of the bowl. Knead for three minutes, adding the extra flour if necessary. Knead by hand on a lightly floured board for one minute or until the dough is no longer sticky.

BY FOOD PROCESSOR

THE NEXT MORNING, place the yeast and water in the food processor bowl fitted with the steel blade. Pulse for 10 seconds to mix. Add the remaining ingredients and almost all of the rye flour and process, with several pulses to mix, for about one minute. Add enough of the remaining flour so that the dough comes together. Knead by hand on a lightly floured board for one minute or until the dough is no longer sticky.

If you have a small food processor, process the dough in two batches and do not overwork dough.

THE NEXT STEP

PLACE THE DOUGH in a lightly oiled bowl and turn dough over so that it is thinly coated on all sides with oil. Put the bowl in a large plastic bag and leave in a warm place until the dough has doubled in size.

PUNCH DOWN and knead for 10 seconds so that the dough is back to its original size. Shape into a round and cut a cross on top with a single edged razor blade or a thin sharp knife. Place on a greased baking tray, cover with a dry cloth and leave to rise until nearly doubled in size again.

PREHEAT OVEN to moderately hot (200°C/400°F).

BRUSH LIGHTLY with cold black coffee and bake for 35 to 40 minutes or until the bread sounds hollow when tapped on the bottom and there is no stale beer smell. Cool on a wire rack.

Fast White Sourdough Bread

15 g (½ oz) fresh yeast or
  1 sachet dried yeast
½ cup water, lukewarm for
  fresh yeast, warm for dried
  yeast
1 cup sourdough starter at
  room temperature (see
  recipe page 76)
2 level teaspoons salt
1 level teaspoon sugar
3 to 3½ cups bread making
  flour or plain (all-purpose)
  flour sifted with 3 level
  teaspoons gluten flour

BY HAND

PLACE THE YEAST in a large mixing bowl, add the water and stir until the yeast dissolves. Add the sourdough starter salt, sugar, and half of the flour and beat very well with a wooden spoon. Add almost all of the remaining flour, a half a cupful at a time. When the dough becomes too stiff for the spoon, use just one floured hand to knead the dough in the bowl.

TURN THE DOUGH onto a lightly floured board and knead for five minutes or until the dough no longer sticks to your hands or the board and it is smooth and elastic. Use just a very light sprinkling of flour on the board to stop the dough from sticking.

BY MIXER

PLACE THE YEAST and water in a large mixer bowl. Stir to dissolve yeast. Add the remaining ingredients and almost all of the flour and mix, using the dough hook and a low speed, until the dough comes together and leaves the sides and bottom of the bowl. Knead for three minutes, adding the extra flour if necessary. Knead by hand on a lightly floured board for one minute or until the dough is no longer sticky.

BY FOOD PROCESSOR

PLACE THE YEAST and water in the food processor bowl fitted with the steel blade. Pulse for 10 seconds to mix. Add the remaining ingredients and almost all of the flour and process, with several pulses to mix, for about one minute. Add enough of the remaining flour so that the dough comes together. Knead by hand on a lightly floured board for one minute or until the dough is no longer sticky.

If you have a small food processor, process the dough in two batches and do not overwork dough.

THE NEXT STEP

PLACE THE DOUGH in a lightly oiled bowl and turn dough over so that it is very thinly coated all over with oil. Put the bowl in a large plastic bag and leave in a warm place until the dough has doubled in size. PUNCH DOWN and knead for 10 seconds so that the dough is back to its original size. Shape into a round and place on a greased baking tray. Dust thickly with flour, cover with a dry cloth and leave to rise in a warm place until doubled in size again; about one to two hours. PREHEAT OVEN to moderately hot (200°C/400°F). BAKE FOR 35 to 40 minutes or until the bread sounds hollow when tapped on the bottom and there is no stale beer smell. Cool on a wire rack.

Fast Wholemeal Sourdough Bread

- 15 g (½ oz) fresh yeast or 1 sachet dried yeast
- ¾ cup water, lukewarm for fresh yeast warm for dried yeast
- 1 cup sourdough starter at room temperature (see recipe page 76)
- 2 level teaspoons salt
- 1 level teaspoon sugar
- 2 cups wholemeal (whole-wheat) flour
- 1 to 1½ cups bread making flour or plain (all-purpose) flour sifted with 1 level teaspoon gluten flour

BY HAND

PLACE THE YEAST in a large mixing bowl, add the water and stir until the yeast dissolves. Add the sourdough starter, salt, sugar, wholemeal flour and half of the bread making flour and beat very well with a wooden spoon. Add almost all of the remaining flour, a half a cupful at a time. When the dough becomes too stiff for the spoon, use just one floured hand to knead the dough in the bowl. TURN THE DOUGH onto a lightly floured board and knead for five minutes or until the dough no longer sticks to your hands or the board and it is smooth and elastic. Use just a very light sprinkling of flour on the board to stop the dough from sticking.

BY MIXER

PLACE THE YEAST and water in a large mixer bowl. Stir to dissolve yeast. Add the remaining ingredients and almost all of the bread making flour and mix, using the dough hook and a low speed, until the dough comes together and leaves the sides and bottom of the bowl. Knead for three minutes, adding the extra flour if necessary. Knead by hand on a lightly floured board for one minute or until the dough is no longer sticky.

BY FOOD PROCESSOR

PLACE THE YEAST and water in the food processor bowl fitted with the steel blade. Pulse for 10 seconds to mix. Add the remaining ingredients and almost all of the bread making flour and process, with several pulses to mix, for about one minute. Add enough of the remaining flour so that the dough comes together. Knead by hand on a lightly floured board for one minute or until the dough is no longer sticky.

If you have a small food processor, process the dough in two batches and do not overwork dough.

THE NEXT STEP

PLACE THE DOUGH in a lightly oiled bowl and turn dough over so that it is very thinly coated all over with oil. Put the bowl in a large plastic bag and leave in a warm place until the dough has doubled in size.

PUNCH DOWN and knead for 10 seconds so that the dough is back to its original size. Shape into a round and place on a greased baking tray. Dust thickly with flour, cover with a dry cloth and leave to rise in a warm place until doubled in size again; about one to two hours.

PREHEAT OVEN to moderately hot (200°C/400°F).

BAKE FOR 35 to 40 minutes or until the bread sounds hollow when tapped on the bottom and there is no stale beer smell. Cool on a wire rack.

Pretend Sourdough Bread

30 g (1 oz) fresh yeast or
  1½ sachets dried yeast
¼ cup water, lukewarm for
  fresh yeast, warm for dried
  yeast
1¼ cups plain yoghurt,
  regular or non-fat, at room
  temperature
2 level teaspoons salt
2 level teaspoons sugar
1 tablespoon oil (if using
  non-fat yoghurt)
3½ to 4 cups bread making
  flour or plain (all-purpose)
  flour sifted with 3 level
  teaspoons gluten flour

BY HAND

PLACE THE YEAST in a large mixing bowl, add the water and stir until the yeast dissolves. Add the yoghurt, salt, sugar, oil and half of the flour and beat very well with a wooden spoon. Add almost all of the remaining flour, a half a cupful at a time. When the dough becomes too stiff for the spoon, use just one floured hand to knead the dough in the bowl.

TURN THE DOUGH onto a lightly floured board and knead for five minutes or until the dough no longer sticks to your hands or the board and it is smooth and elastic. Use just a very light sprinkling of flour on the board to stop the dough from sticking.

BY MIXER

PLACE THE YEAST and water in a large mixer bowl. Stir to dissolve yeast. Add the remaining ingredients and almost all of the flour and mix, using the dough hook and a low speed, until the dough comes together and leaves the sides and bottom of the bowl. Knead for three minutes, adding the extra flour if necessary. Knead by hand on a lightly floured board for one minute or until the dough is no longer sticky.

BY FOOD PROCESSOR

PLACE THE YEAST and water in the food processor bowl fitted with the steel blade. Pulse for 10 seconds to mix. Add the remaining ingredients and almost all of the flour and process, with several pulses to mix, for about one minute. Add enough of the remaining flour so that the dough comes together. Knead by hand on a lightly floured board for one minute or until the dough is no longer sticky.

If you have a small food processor, process the dough in two batches and do not overwork dough.

THE NEXT STEP

PLACE THE DOUGH in a lightly oiled bowl and turn dough over so that it is very thinly coated all over with oil. Put the bowl in a large plastic bag and leave in a warm place until the dough has doubled in size.

PUNCH DOWN and knead for 10 seconds so that the dough is back to its original size. Shape into a round and place on a greased baking tray. Cover with a dry cloth and leave to rise until nearly doubled in size again.

PREHEAT OVEN to moderately hot (200°C/400°F).

BAKE FOR 35 to 40 minutes or until the bread sounds hollow

when tapped on the bottom and there is no stale beer smell. Cool on a wire rack.

This is really a cheating way to produce a sourdough but I have fooled some with it.

FLATBREADS

Pita Bread

20 g (¾ oz) fresh yeast or
  1 sachet dried yeast
1¼ cups water, lukewarm
  for fresh, warm for dried
1 level teaspoon salt
1 level teaspoon sugar
3½ to 4 cups bread making
  flour or plain (all-purpose)
  flour sifted with 3
  teaspoons gluten flour

BY HAND
PLACE THE YEAST in a large mixing bowl, add the water and stir until the yeast dissolves. Add the salt, sugar and half of the flour and beat very well with a wooden spoon. Add almost all of the remaining flour, a half a cupful at a time. When the dough becomes too stiff for the spoon, use just one floured hand to knead the dough in the bowl.

TURN THE DOUGH onto a lightly floured board and knead for five minutes or until the dough no longer sticks to your hands or the board and it is smooth and elastic. Use just a very light sprinkling of flour on the board to stop the dough from sticking.

BY MIXER
PLACE THE YEAST and water in a large mixer bowl. Stir to dissolve yeast. Add the remaining ingredients and almost all of the flour and mix, using the dough hook and a low speed, until the dough comes together and leaves the sides and bottom of the bowl. Knead for three minutes, adding the extra flour if necessary. Knead by hand on a lightly floured board for one minute or until the dough is no longer sticky.

BY FOOD PROCESSOR
PLACE THE YEAST and water in the food processor bowl fitted with the steel blade. Pulse for 10 seconds to mix. Add the remaining ingredients and almost all of the flour and process, with several pulses to mix, for about one minute. Add enough of the remaining flour so that the dough comes together. Knead by hand on a lightly floured board for one minute or until the dough is no longer sticky.

If you have a small food processor, process the dough in two batches and do not overwork dough.

THE NEXT STEP
PLACE THE DOUGH in a lightly oiled bowl and turn dough over so that it is very thinly coated all over with oil. Put the bowl in a large plastic

bag and leave in a warm place until the dough has doubled in size.

SET OVEN to its hottest setting, about (250°C/475°F).

PUNCH DOWN and knead the dough for 10 seconds so that it is back to its original size. Divide the dough into 12 equal pieces and shape into balls. Cover the dough balls with a dry cloth and leave for 10 minutes. After 10 minutes take out 2 of the balls and leave the others covered. Roll the two balls as thinly as possible, without creasing the dough.

PLACE ON an ungreased baking tray and bake in the preheated oven, set at its hottest setting, for five to seven minutes or until the breads are puffed up and cooked. Repeat the procedure with the remaining dough. Eat immediately or store, when completely cold, in a plastic bag to keep soft.

It's always exciting peering through the glass window of my oven watching to see if these are going to puff up and create a pocket inside that can be filled. They cook very quickly in the hottest of ovens and you need to be careful not to open the door too wide so that the heat does not escape. And only cook two at a time.

Naan

20 g (¾ oz) fresh yeast or
  1 sachet dried yeast
¾ cup water, lukewarm for
  fresh yeast, warm for dried
3 level teaspoons sugar
2 level teaspoons salt
¼ cup plain yoghurt or
  buttermilk, at room
  temperature
1 egg, lightly beaten
¼ cup melted butter or
  ghee (clarified butter)
3½ to 4 cups bread making
  flour or plain (all-purpose)
  flour sifted with 3 level
  teaspoons gluten flour
      extra melted butter

GLAZE AND DECORATION
plain yoghurt or buttermilk
poppyseeds or black cumin
seeds or caraway seeds

BY HAND

PLACE THE YEAST in a large mixing bowl, add the water and stir until the yeast dissolves. Mix in the sugar, salt, yoghurt, egg and the butter. Add half of the flour and beat very well with a spoon. Add the remaining flour, a little at a time. When the dough becomes too stiff for the spoon, use just one floured hand to knead the dough in the bowl.

KNEAD, using a pulling and slapping action, for 10 minutes or until the dough no longer sticks to your fingers. Naan dough is meant to be very soft and moist so add only a little of the remaining flour.

From time to time clean your hand with a scraper and re-flour. Scrape down the dough from the sides of the bowl and brush the top lightly with a little melted butter.

BY MIXER

PLACE THE YEAST and water in a large mixer bowl. Stir to dissolve yeast. Add the remaining ingredients and almost all of the flour and mix, using the dough hook and a low speed, for three minutes. Scrape down the dough from the sides of the bowl and brush the top lightly with a little melted butter.

BY FOOD PROCESSOR

PLACE THE YEAST and water in the food processor bowl fitted with the steel blade. Pulse for 10 seconds to mix. Add the remaining ingredients and almost all of the flour and process, with several pulses to mix, for about one minute. Add enough of the remaining flour so that the dough just comes together. Brush the top lightly with a little melted butter.

If you only have a small food processor, process the dough in two batches and do not overwork dough.

THE NEXT STEP

PLACE THE BOWL in a large plastic bag and then in a warm place and leave until the dough has doubled in size. Preheat oven to hottest setting and heat ungreased thin baking trays.

PUNCH DOWN the dough and knead lightly for 10 seconds so that the dough is back to its original size. Use very well floured hands to divide and shape the dough into 10 roughly equal balls. Place each ball on a very well floured board and flatten into a round, 6 mm (1/4 in) thick, and then pull one end outwards to make a pear shape. Brush with yoghurt and sprinkle with the seeds.

PLACE TWO OR THREE at a time on the preheated trays and bake in the preheated oven for about eight minutes or until the bottom of the bread is dark brown. Serve immediately.

Indian meals are made even more wonderful with naan. It's more authentic to bake in a clay tandoor oven but you can bake very adequately in a normal oven. If you like, you can add a handful of sultanas and grated fresh coconut to make an exotic and delicious variation.

The Rolls and Buns

Shaping and Baking Rolls

PAN ROLLS

SHAPE THE DOUGH into balls about 4 cm (1½ in) in diameter. Place in a greased 20 cm (8 in) pan so that the sides just touch. Brush lightly with butter, cover with a cloth and let rise in a warm place until doubled in size.

BAKE IN a moderately hot oven (200°C/400°F) for 10 to 12 minutes or until golden brown. Turn out of pan to cool on a wire rack.

FINGER ROLLS

DIVIDE THE DOUGH into pieces about the size of walnuts. Shape each piece into a roll about 10 cm (4 in) long and place in a greased 20 cm (8 in) pan with the sides just touching. Brush lightly with butter, cover with a cloth and let rise in a warm place until doubled in size.

BAKE IN a moderately hot oven (200°C/400°F) for 10 to 12 minutes or until golden brown. Turn out of pan to cool on a wire rack.

CRESCENTS

DIVIDE THE DOUGH in half and roll each half into a circle about 6 mm (¼ in) thick. Cut the circle of dough into wedges 10 cm (4 in) across at the wide end. Starting at a wide end, roll up each wedge towards the point. Place point side down on a greased baking tray. Curve ends, to make a crescent shape, and brush with beaten egg yolk. Cover with a cloth and let rise in a warm place until doubled in size.

BAKE IN a moderately hot oven (200°C/400°F) for 15 to 20 minutes or until golden brown. Cool on a wire rack.

CLOVERLEAF ROLLS

SHAPE DOUGH into small balls about 2.5 cm (1 in) in diameter. Grease a deep muffin tray and place three balls in each muffin cup. Brush lightly with melted butter, cover with a cloth and let rise in a warm place until doubled in size.

BAKE IN a moderately hot oven (200°C/400°F) for 10 to 15 minutes or until golden brown. Turn out of pan to cool on a wire rack.

BOWS

DIVIDE THE DOUGH into pieces the size of walnuts. With buttered hands gently roll and shape into 20 cm (8 in) strips. Tie into loose knots and place on a greased baking tray. Cover with a cloth and let rise until doubled in size. Bake in a moderately hot oven (200°C/400°F) for 10 to 15 minutes or until golden brown. Cool on a wire rack.

FIGURE EIGHTS

DIVIDE THE DOUGH into pieces the size of walnuts. With buttered hands gently roll and shape into 20 cm (8 in) strips. Join ends of dough and twist into a figure eight (8) shape. Cover with a cloth and let rise until doubled in size.
Bake in a moderately hot oven (200°C/400°F) for 10 to 15 minutes or until golden brown. Cool on a wire rack.

PINWHEELS

FLATTEN THE DOUGH into a 22 x 45 cm (9 x 18 in) rectangle. Brush with melted butter. Roll up like a Swiss (jelly) roll, starting at a long side. Cut into 2.5 cm (1 in) slices and place, cut side down, on a greased baking tray. Cover with a cloth and let rise until doubled in size.
BAKE IN a moderately hot oven (200°C/400°F) for 10 to 15 minutes or until golden brown. Cool on a wire rack.

PLAITS (BRAIDS)

FLATTEN THE DOUGH and roll out to 60 mm (¼ in) thickness. Cut into 1.25 x 12 cm (½ x 5 in) strips. Plait strips together in groups of three and seal the ends. Place on a greased baking tray and brush tops lightly with beaten egg. Sprinkle with sesame seeds. Cover with a cloth and let rise until doubled in size.
BAKE IN a moderately hot oven (200°C/400°F) for 10 to 15 minutes or until golden brown. Cool on a wire rack.

Serving homemade bread rolls for dinner guests often rates more undeserved praise than the main meal and, for an outrageous touch, shape the dough into your initials.

Soft Dinner Rolls

20 g (¾ oz) fresh yeast or
  1 sachet dried yeast
¼ cup water, lukewarm for
  fresh yeast, warm for dried
  yeast
½ cup milk, lukewarm for
  fresh yeast, warm for dried
  yeast
1 level teaspoon salt
¼ cup sugar
¼ cup oil or melted butter
1 egg at room temperature,
  lightly beaten
3½ to 4 cups bread making
  flour or plain (all-purpose)
  flour sifted with 3 level
  teaspoons gluten flour

GLAZE
milk

BY HAND

PLACE THE YEAST in a large mixing bowl, add the water and stir until the yeast dissolves. Add the milk, salt, sugar, oil, egg and half of the flour and beat very well with a wooden spoon. Add almost all of the remaining flour, a half a cupful at a time. When the dough becomes too stiff for the spoon, use just one floured hand to knead the dough in the bowl.

TURN THE DOUGH onto a lightly floured board and knead for five minutes or until the dough no longer sticks to your hands or the board and it is smooth and elastic. Use just a very light sprinkling of flour on the board to stop the dough from sticking.

BY MIXER

PLACE THE YEAST and water in a large mixer bowl. Stir to dissolve yeast. Add the remaining ingredients and almost all of the flour and mix, using the dough hook and a low speed, until the dough comes together and leaves the sides and bottom of the bowl. Knead for three minutes, adding the extra flour if necessary. Knead by hand on a lightly floured board for one minute or until the dough is no longer sticky.

BY FOOD PROCESSOR

PLACE THE YEAST and water in the food processor bowl fitted with the steel blade. Pulse for 10 seconds to mix. Add the remaining ingredients and almost all of the flour and process, with several pulses to mix, for about one minute. Add enough of the remaining flour so that the dough comes together. Knead by hand on a lightly floured board for one minute or until the dough is no longer sticky.

If you have a small food processor, process the dough in two batches and do not overwork dough.

THE NEXT STEP

PLACE THE DOUGH in a lightly oiled bowl and turn dough over so that it is very thinly coated all over with oil. Put the bowl in a large plastic bag and leave in a warm place until the dough has doubled in size.

PUNCH DOWN and knead for 10 seconds so that the dough is back to its original size. Shape as desired and let rise again, covered with a dry cloth. Brush lightly with milk. Bake in a preheated oven.(Refer Shaping and Baking Rolls page 88.)

Wholemeal Dinner Rolls

20 g (¾ oz) fresh yeast or
  1 sachet dried yeast
½ cup water, lukewarm for
  fresh yeast, warm for dried
  yeast
½ cup milk, lukewarm for
  fresh yeast, warm for dried
  yeast
1 level teaspoon salt
¼ cup sugar
¼ cup oil or melted butter
1 egg at room temperature,
  lightly beaten
2 cups wholemeal (whole-
  wheat) flour
1½ to 2 cups bread making
  flour or plain (all-purpose)
  flour sifted with 2 level
  teaspoons gluten flour

BY HAND

PLACE THE YEAST in a large mixing bowl, add the water and stir until the yeast dissolves. Add the milk, salt, sugar, oil, egg and the wholemeal flour and beat very well with a wooden spoon. Add almost all of the bread making flour, a half a cupful at a time. When the dough becomes too stiff for the spoon, use just one floured hand to knead the dough in the bowl.

TURN THE DOUGH onto a lightly floured board and knead for five minutes or until the dough no longer sticks to your hands or the board and it is smooth and elastic. Use just a very light sprinkling of flour on the board to stop the dough from sticking.

BY MIXER

PLACE THE YEAST and water in a large mixer bowl. Stir to dissolve yeast. Add the remaining ingredients and almost all of the bread making flour and mix, using the dough hook and a low speed, until the dough comes together and leaves the sides and bottom of the bowl. Knead for three minutes, adding the extra flour if necessary. Knead by hand on a lightly floured board for one minute or until the dough is no longer sticky.

BY FOOD PROCESSOR

PLACE THE YEAST and water in the food processor bowl fitted with the steel blade. Pulse for 10 seconds to mix. Add the remaining ingredients and almost all of the bread making flour and process, with several pulses to mix, for about one minute. Add enough of the remaining flour so that the dough comes together. Knead by hand on a lightly floured board for one minute or until the dough is no longer sticky.

If you have a small food processor, process the dough in two batches and do not overwork dough.

THE NEXT STEP

PLACE THE DOUGH in a lightly oiled bowl and turn dough over so that it is very thinly coated all over with oil. Put the bowl in a large plastic bag and leave in a warm place until the dough has doubled in size.

PUNCH DOWN and knead for 10 seconds so that the dough is back to its original size. Shape as desired (refer Shaping and Baking Rolls page 88) and let rise again, covered with a dry cloth.

PREHEAT OVEN to moderately hot (200°C/400°F).

BAKE FOR 10 to 15 minutes or until golden brown. Cool on a wire rack.

Hamburger Buns with Sesame Seeds

20 g (¾ oz) fresh yeast or
  1 sachet dried yeast
¼ cup water, lukewarm for
  fresh yeast, warm for dried
  yeast
¾ cup milk, lukewarm for
  fresh yeast, warm for dried
  yeast
1 level teaspoon salt
1 level tablespoon sugar
½ cup oil or melted butter
3½ to 4 cups bread making
  flour or plain (all-purpose)
  flour sifted with 3 level
  teaspoons gluten flour

GLAZE AND DECORATION
water
sesame seeds

BY HAND

PLACE THE YEAST in a large mixing bowl, add the water and stir until the yeast dissolves. Add the milk, salt, sugar, oil and half of the flour and beat very well with a wooden spoon. Add almost all of the remaining flour, a half a cupful at a time. When the dough becomes too stiff for the spoon, use just one floured hand to knead the dough in the bowl.

TURN THE DOUGH onto a lightly floured board and knead for five minutes or until the dough no longer sticks to your hands or the board and it is smooth and elastic. Use just a very light sprinkling of flour on the board to stop the dough from sticking.

BY MIXER

PLACE THE YEAST and water in a large mixer bowl. Stir to dissolve yeast. Add the remaining ingredients and almost all of the flour and mix, using the dough hook and a low speed, until the dough comes together and leaves the sides and bottom of the bowl. Knead for three minutes, adding the extra flour if necessary. Knead by hand on a lightly floured board for one minute or until the dough is no longer sticky.

BY FOOD PROCESSOR

PLACE THE YEAST and water in the food processor bowl fitted with the steel blade. Pulse for 10 seconds to mix. Add the remaining ingredients and almost all of the flour and process, with several pulses to mix, for about one minute. Add enough of the remaining flour so that the dough comes together. Knead by hand on a lightly floured board for one minute or until the dough is no longer sticky.

If you have a small food processor, process the dough in two batches and do not overwork dough.

THE NEXT STEP

PLACE THE DOUGH in a lightly oiled bowl and turn dough over so that it is very thinly coated all over with oil. Put the bowl in a large plastic bag and leave in a warm place until the dough has doubled in size.

PUNCH DOWN and knead for 10 seconds so that the dough is back to its original size. Knead in a little extra flour if necessary to make a firm dough. Roll or flatten the dough to 1.25 cm (½ in) thickness. Cut into rounds with a 10 cm (4 in) cutter.

RIGHT: *Tea Ring using sweet orange dough (page 110)*

PLACE THE DOUGH on a greased baking tray, 10 cm (4 in) apart, and spray lightly with water. Sprinkle on the sesame seeds. Cover with a cloth and let rise until doubled in size.

PREHEAT OVEN to moderately hot (200°C/400°F).

BAKE FOR 15 to 20 minutes or until golden brown and there is no stale beer smell. Cool on a wire rack.

These are those quite famous sesame seed buns to be found on the outside of hamburgers. To keep them soft, store in a sealed plastic bag as soon as they have cooled completely.

Croissants

*20 g (¾ oz) fresh yeast or
  1 sachet dried yeast*
*¼ cup water, lukewarm for
  fresh yeast, warm for dried
  yeast*
*²/₃ cup milk, lukewarm for
  fresh yeast, warm for dried
  yeast*
2 level teaspoons salt
1 level tablespoon sugar
¼ cup oil
*2 eggs at room temperature,
  lightly beaten*
*3½ to 4 cups bread making
  flour or plain (all-purpose)
  flour sifted with 3
  teaspoons gluten flour*
1 cup soft unsalted butter

GLAZE
beaten egg with a little water

Makes 12

BY HAND

PLACE THE YEAST in a large mixing bowl, add the water and stir until the yeast dissolves. Add the milk, salt, sugar, oil, eggs and half of the flour and beat very well with a wooden spoon. Add almost all of the remaining flour, a half a cupful at a time. When the dough becomes too stiff for the spoon, use just one floured hand to knead the dough in the bowl.

TURN THE DOUGH onto a lightly floured board and knead for five minutes or until the dough no longer sticks to your hands or the board and it is smooth and elastic. Use just a very light sprinkling of flour on the board to stop the dough from sticking.

BY MIXER

PLACE THE YEAST and water in a large mixer bowl. Stir to dissolve yeast. Add the remaining ingredients, except the unsalted butter, and almost all of the flour. Mix, using the dough hook and a low speed, until the dough comes together and leaves the sides and bottom of the bowl. Knead for three minutes, adding the extra flour if necessary. Knead by hand on a lightly floured board for one minute or until the dough is no longer sticky.

BY FOOD PROCESSOR

PLACE THE YEAST and water in the food processor bowl fitted with the steel blade. Pulse for 10 seconds to mix. Add the remaining ingredients, except the unsalted butter, and almost all of the flour. Process, with several pulses to mix, for about one minute. Add enough of the remaining flour so that the dough comes together. Knead by hand on a lightly floured board for one minute or until the dough is no longer sticky.

LEFT: *Chelsea Buns (page 112)*

If you have a small food processor, process the dough in two batches and do not overwork dough.

THE NEXT STEP

PLACE THE DOUGH in a lightly oiled bowl and turn dough over so that it is very thinly coated all over with oil. Put the bowl in a large plastic bag and leave in a warm place until the dough has doubled in size.

PUNCH DOWN and knead for 10 seconds so that the dough is back to its original size. Place the dough back in its bowl, cover and refrigerate for one hour.

PUNCH DOWN AGAIN and roll the dough into a large rectangle about 25 x 60 cm (10 x 24 in). Divide the softened butter into three equal portions and spread one portion all over the dough.

FOLD THE DOUGH crosswise into three to make a shape about 25 x 20 cm (10 x 8 in). Roll out to make another large rectangle and spread with another third of the butter. Fold again and repeat the rolling and then the spreading of the last third of the butter. Fold the dough into three, as before, and cover with plastic film. Refrigerate for one hour.

DIVIDE THE DOUGH in half and roll into a large 40 cm (16 in) circle. Cut the dough into halves, then quarters and then each quarter into three. Roll up each triangular wedge, starting at a long side, and place on an ungreased baking tray, with the points underneath. Shape into crescents.

In hot summer weather, chill croissants in the refrigerator for 30 minutes. In cold winter weather cover croissants with a dry cloth and leave in a cool place for 30 minutes.

PREHEAT OVEN to hot (220°C/425°F).

BRUSH CROISSANTS with beaten egg glaze and bake for 15 to 20 minutes or until golden brown. Cool on a wire rack.

Believe it or not, this is a very simple recipe for croissants; others can be much, much, much more complicated. Croissants freeze very well so there is really no need to get up in the middle of the night to make them for breakfast. And, the amount of praise you get for homemade croissants is ridiculous.

Bagels

20 g (¾ oz) fresh yeast or
  1 sachet dried yeast
1 cup milk, lukewarm for
  fresh yeast, warm for dried
  yeast
½ level teaspoon salt
2 level tablespoons sugar
¼ cup melted butter or oil
1 egg white, at room
  temperature, lightly beaten
3½ to 4 cups bread making
  flour or plain (all-purpose)
  flour sifted with 3 level
  teaspoons gluten flour

FOR PRECOOKING
boiling water
2 more tablespoons salt for
  savoury bagels or 2 more
  tablespoons sugar for sweet
  bagels

GLAZE AND DECORATION
1 egg yolk beaten with 1
  teaspoon water
poppyseeds or sesame seeds
  or rock salt crystals

BY HAND
PLACE THE YEAST in a large mixing bowl, add the milk and stir until the yeast dissolves. Add the salt, sugar, butter, egg white, and half the flour and beat very well with a wooden spoon. Add almost all of the remaining flour, a half a cupful at a time. When the dough becomes too stiff for the spoon, use just one floured hand to knead the dough in the bowl.

TURN THE DOUGH onto a lightly floured board and knead for five minutes or until the dough no longer sticks to your hands or the board and it is smooth and elastic. Use just a very light sprinkling of flour on the board to stop the dough from sticking.

BY MIXER
PLACE THE YEAST and milk in a large mixer bowl. Stir to dissolve yeast. Add the remaining ingredients and almost all of the flour and mix, using the dough hook and a low speed, until the dough comes together and leaves the sides and bottom of the bowl. Knead for three minutes, adding the extra flour if necessary. Knead by hand on a lightly floured board for one minute or until the dough is no longer sticky.

BY FOOD PROCESSOR
PLACE THE YEAST and milk in the food processor bowl fitted with the steel blade. Pulse for 10 seconds to mix. Add the remaining ingredients and almost all of the flour and process, with several pulses to mix, for about one minute. Add enough of the remaining flour so that the dough comes together. Knead by hand on a lightly floured board for one minute or until the dough is no longer sticky.

If you have a small food processor, process the dough in two batches and do not overwork dough.

THE NEXT STEP
PLACE THE DOUGH in a lightly oiled bowl and turn dough over so that it is thinly coated all over with oil. Put the bowl in a large plastic bag and leave in a warm place until the dough has doubled in size. PUNCH DOWN and knead for 10 seconds so that the dough is back to its original size. Divide the dough into eight pieces and shape each into a ball. To make the bagel shape, push both thumbs completely through the centre of the dough and stretch and twist the dough to make a large ring. Cover with a dry cloth and leave for 10 minutes. BRING A LARGE wide pan of water to the boil, add the extra salt or extra sugar, depending on the flavour you want the crust to have.

Turn down the heat, so the water is gently simmering, and lower the bagels, a few at a time, into the water. Turn the bagels over as they come to the surface and cook for three minutes. Lift out with an egg slice and drain very, very well.

PREHEAT OVEN to moderately hot (200°C/400°F).

PLACE ON a greased baking tray and brush with the beaten egg yolk and water. Sprinkle with the poppyseeds or sesame seeds or salt crystals. Bake for 20 minutes or until golden brown. Lift the bagels off the baking tray and cool on a wire rack.

These come close to some of the bagels I ate in New York with cream cheese and jelly for breakfast and they are much better than many of the bagels I've eaten in Sydney.

Blueberry Bagels

20 g (¾ oz) fresh yeast or
  1 sachet dried yeast
1 cup milk, lukewarm for
  fresh yeast, warm for dried
  yeast
½ level teaspoon salt
½ level teaspoon ground
  cinnamon
2 level tablespoons sugar
¼ cup melted butter or oil
1 egg white at room
  temperature
3½ to 4 cups bread making
  flour or plain (all-purpose)
  flour sifted with 3 level
  teaspoons gluten flour
½ cup fresh or thawed
  frozen blueberries

FOR PRECOOKING
boiling water
2 tablespoons extra sugar

GLAZE
1 egg yolk beaten with 1
teaspoon water

BY HAND

PLACE THE YEAST in a large mixing bowl, add the milk and stir until the yeast dissolves. Add the salt, cinnamon, sugar, butter, egg white and half the flour and beat very well with a wooden spoon. Add almost all of the remaining flour, a half a cupful at a time. When the dough becomes too stiff for the spoon, use just one floured hand to knead the dough in the bowl.

TURN THE DOUGH onto a lightly floured board and knead for five minutes or until the dough no longer sticks to your hands or the board and the dough is smooth and elastic. Use just a very light sprinkling of flour on the board to stop the dough from sticking.

BY MIXER

PLACE THE YEAST and water in a large mixer bowl. Stir to dissolve yeast. Add the remaining ingredients, except blueberries, and almost all of the flour. Mix, using the dough hook and a low speed, until the dough comes together and leaves the sides and bottom of the bowl. Knead for three minutes, adding the extra flour if necessary. Knead by hand on a lightly floured board for one minute or until the dough is no longer sticky.

BY FOOD PROCESSOR

PLACE THE YEAST and water in the food processor bowl fitted with the steel blade. Pulse for 10 seconds to mix. Add the remaining ingredients, except blueberries, and almost all of the flour.

Process, with several pulses to mix, for about one minute. Add enough of the remaining flour so that the dough comes together. Knead by hand on a lightly floured board for one minute or until the dough is no longer sticky.

If you have a small food processor, process the dough in two batches and do not overwork dough.

THE NEXT STEP

PLACE THE DOUGH in a lightly oiled bowl and turn dough over so that it is thinly coated all over with oil. Put the bowl in a large plastic bag and leave in a warm place until the dough has doubled in size.

PUNCH DOWN and knead for 10 seconds so that the dough is back to its original size. Knead in the blueberries very gently. Divide the dough into eight pieces and shape each into a ball. To make the bagel shape, push both thumbs completely through the centre of the dough and stretch and twist the dough to make a large ring.

COVER WITH a dry cloth and leave for 10 minutes.

BRING A LARGE wide pan of water to the boil and add the extra sugar. Turn down the heat, so the water is gently simmering, and lower the bagels, a few at a time, into the water. Turn the bagels over as they come to the surface and cook for three minutes. Lift out with an egg slice and drain very, very well.

PREHEAT OVEN to moderately hot (200°C/400°F).

PLACE THE BAGELS on a greased baking tray and brush with the beaten egg yolk and water. Bake for 20 minutes or until golden brown. Lift the bagels off the baking tray and cool on a wire rack.

I know that fresh blueberries would be much better in these bagels than the frozen ones but, as I always eat them before I get around to Blueberry Bagel baking, I now buy the frozen ones.

Breakfast Rolls

20 g (¾ oz) fresh yeast or
  1 sachet dried yeast
½ cup water, lukewarm for
  fresh yeast, warm for dried
  yeast
½ cup milk, lukewarm for
  fresh yeast, warm for dried
  yeast
1 level teaspoon salt
¼ cup sugar
2 tablespoons oil
1 egg at room temperature,
  lightly beaten
3¼ to 3½ cups bread
  making or plain (all-
  purpose) flour sifted with 3
  level teaspoons gluten flour
  extra oil

GLAZE AND DECORATION
milk
flour

BY HAND

PLACE THE YEAST in a large mixing bowl, add the water and milk
and stir until the yeast dissolves. Mix in the salt, sugar, oil and egg.
Add half the flour and beat very well with a spoon. Add the remaining flour, a little at a time, to make a very soft dough. Brush
the top of the dough with a little oil and put the bowl in a large
plastic bag and refrigerate overnight.

BY MIXER

PLACE THE YEAST and water in a large mixer bowl. Stir to dissolve
yeast. Add the remaining ingredients and almost all of the flour and
mix, using the dough hook and a low speed, until the dough comes
together and leaves the sides and bottom of the bowl. Knead for
three minutes, adding the extra flour if necessary to make a very
soft dough. Brush the top of the dough with a little oil and put the
bowl in a large plastic bag and refrigerate overnight.

BY FOOD PROCESSOR

PLACE THE YEAST and water in the food processor bowl fitted with
the steel blade. Pulse for 10 seconds to mix. Add the remaining
ingredients and almost all of the flour and process, with several pulses
to mix, for about one minute. Add enough of the remaining flour to
make a very soft dough. Brush the top of the dough with a little oil
and put the bowl in a large plastic bag and refrigerate overnight.

THE NEXT STEP

NEXT MORNING knead the dough lightly with floured hands until
it is back to its original size. Divide the dough into eight flat ovals.
Place on a greased baking tray and flatten each piece of dough.
BRUSH THE TOPS with milk and sprinkle lightly with flour. Place
in a *cold* oven and turn the temperature control to moderately hot
(200°C/400°F).
BAKE FOR 20 to 25 minutes or until there is no stale beer smell.
Serve immediately.

These are not the most wonderful of rolls but it is a way to have
freshly made bread rolls for breakfast without getting up before
dawn to make them. The dough is made the evening before, rises
in the refrigerator overnight and in the morning is shaped into
rolls, placed in a **cold** oven and baked without waiting for second
rising. Everyone is impressed when they wake with the smell of
freshly baking bread and, if you serve them immediately with lots
of butter and jam, they'll think the taste is great too.

Wholemeal Bread Rolls

½ cup cracked wheat grains
2 cups boiling water
20 g (¾ oz) fresh yeast or
  1 sachet dried yeast
1 level teaspoon salt
1 tablespoon light honey or
1½ tablespoons brown
  sugar
1 tablespoon oil or melted
  butter
½ cup wheat germ
2 cups wholemeal (whole-
  wheat) flour
1 to 1½ cups bread making
  flour or plain (all-purpose)
  flour sifted with 1
  teaspoon gluten flour

Pour the boiling water over the cracked wheat grains and leave to cool to lukewarm for fresh yeast and warm for dried yeast. Strain and re-measure water and add to make up to 1° cups.

BY HAND
PLACE THE YEAST in a large mixing bowl, add the water and stir until the yeast dissolves. Add the salt, honey, oil, cooled cracked wheat, wheat germ and half of each flour and beat very well with a wooden spoon. Add almost all of the remaining flour, a half a cupful at a time. When the dough becomes too stiff for the spoon, use just one floured hand to knead the dough in the bowl.
TURN THE DOUGH onto a lightly floured board and knead for five minutes or until the dough no longer sticks to your hands or the board and it is smooth and elastic. Use just a very light sprinkling of flour on the board to stop the dough from sticking.

BY MIXER
PLACE THE YEAST and water in a large mixer bowl. Stir to dissolve yeast. Add the remaining ingredients and almost all of each flour and mix, using the dough hook and a low speed, until the dough comes together and leaves the sides and bottom of the bowl. Knead for three minutes, adding the extra flour if necessary. Knead by hand on a lightly floured board for one minute or until the dough is no longer sticky.

BY FOOD PROCESSOR
PLACE THE YEAST and water in the food processor bowl fitted with the steel blade. Pulse for 10 seconds to mix. Add the remaining ingredients and almost all of each flour and process, with several pulses to mix, for about one minute. Add enough of the remaining flour so that the dough comes together. Knead by hand on a lightly floured board for one minute or until the dough is no longer sticky.

If you have a small food processor, process the dough in two batches and do not overwork dough.

THE NEXT STEP
PLACE THE DOUGH in a lightly oiled bowl and turn dough over so that it is very thinly coated all over with oil. Put the bowl in a large plastic bag and leave in a warm place until the dough has doubled in size.
PUNCH DOWN and knead for 10 seconds so that the dough is back to its original size. Divide the dough into 12 equal pieces and

shape each into a round roll. Flatten slightly with the palm of your hand and place on a greased baking tray. Cover with a dry cloth and leave to rise in a warm place until doubled in size.

PREHEAT OVEN to moderately hot (200°C/400°F).

BAKE FOR 20 to 25 minutes or until there is no stale beer smell. Cool on a wire rack.

You can use all wholemeal (whole-wheat) flour in these bread rolls if you like but the baked rolls will be very heavy and make for very serious eating.

The Cakes and Celebration Breads

Yeast cakes are surprisingly simple to make and you can create your own cake with these 'mix 'n match' recipes.

For the simplest cake, take your pick of any of the doughs. Make the dough, let it rise and then press into a greased pan. Sprinkle with a topping, let it rise again and then bake.

Or find out just how easy shaping sweet doughs is by spreading the rolled out risen dough with a filling, roll it up and then cut it into wonderfully impressive and elaborate shapes.

Basic Sweet Dough

20 g (¾ oz) fresh yeast or
  1 sachet dried yeast
½ cup water, lukewarm for
  fresh yeast, warm for dried
  yeast
½ cup milk, lukewarm for
  fresh yeast, warm for dried
1 level teaspoon salt
¹/₃ cup sugar
¹/₃ cup melted butter or
  margarine
1 egg, at room temperature,
  slightly beaten
3½ to 4 cups bread making
  flour or plain (all-purpose)
  flour sifted with 3 level
  teaspoons gluten flour

BY HAND

PLACE THE YEAST in a large mixing bowl, add the water and stir until the yeast dissolves. Add the milk, salt, sugar, melted butter, egg and half of the flour and beat very well with a wooden spoon. Add almost all of the remaining flour, a half a cupful at a time. When the dough becomes too stiff for the spoon, use just one floured hand to knead the dough in the bowl.

TURN THE DOUGH onto a lightly floured board and knead for five minutes or until the dough no longer sticks to your hands or the board and it is smooth and elastic. Use just a very light sprinkling of flour on the board to stop the dough from sticking.

BY MIXER

PLACE THE YEAST and water in a large mixer bowl. Stir to dissolve yeast. Add the remaining ingredients and almost all of the flour and mix, using the dough hook and a low speed, until the dough comes together and leaves the sides and bottom of the bowl. Knead for three minutes, adding the extra flour if necessary. Knead by hand on a lightly floured board for one minute or until the dough is no longer sticky.

BY FOOD PROCESSOR

PLACE THE YEAST and water in the food processor bowl fitted with the steel blade. Pulse for 10 seconds to mix. Add the remaining ingredients and almost all of the flour and process, with several pulses to mix, for about one minute. Add enough of the remaining flour so that the dough comes together. Knead by hand on a lightly floured board for one minute or until the dough is no longer sticky. If you have a small food processor, process the dough in two batches and do not overwork dough.

THE NEXT STEP

PLACE THE DOUGH in a lightly oiled bowl and turn dough over so that it is very thinly coated all over with oil. Put the bowl in a large plastic bag and leave in a warm place until the dough has doubled in size.

PUNCH DOWN and knead for 10 seconds so that the dough is back to its original size. Shape and let rise, covered with a dry cloth, until doubled in size. Bake in a preheated oven. (Refer to The Simplest, Speediest Way with Sweet Doughs page 106.)

Use this basic sweet dough to make any sort of sweet bread or cake. You vary it completely by using different fillings, different shapes and different glazes.

Brown Sugar Dough

30 g (1 oz) fresh yeast or
  1½ sachets dried yeast
¾ cup water, lukewarm for
  fresh yeast, warm for dried
½ cup milk, lukewarm for
  fresh yeast, warm for dried
  yeast
1 level teaspoon salt
¼ cup brown sugar, firmly
  packed into cup
½ cup melted butter or
  margarine
2 eggs, at room temperature,
  slightly beaten
1 cup uncooked instant
  rolled oats
3 to 3½ cups bread making
  flour or plain (all-purpose)
  flour sifted with 3 level
  teaspoons gluten flour

BY HAND

PLACE THE YEAST in a large mixing bowl, add the water and stir until the yeast dissolves. Add the milk, salt, sugar, butter, eggs, rolled oats and half of the flour and beat very well with a wooden spoon. Add almost all of the remaining flour, a half a cupful at a time. When the dough becomes too stiff for the spoon, use just one floured hand to knead the dough in the bowl.

TURN THE DOUGH onto a lightly floured board and knead for five minutes or until the dough no longer sticks to your hands or the board and it is smooth and elastic. Use just a very light sprinkling of flour on the board to stop the dough from sticking.

BY MIXER

PLACE THE YEAST and water in a large mixer bowl. Stir to dissolve the yeast. Add remaining ingredients and almost all the flour and mix, using the dough hook and a low speed, until the dough comes together and leaves the sides and bottom of the bowl. Knead for three minutes, adding extra flour if necessary. Knead by hand for one minute or until dough is no longer sticky.

BY FOOD PROCESSOR

PLACE THE YEAST and water in the food processor bowl fitted with the steel blade. Pulse for 10 seconds to mix. Add the remaining ingredients and almost all of the flour and process, with several pulses to mix, for about one minute. Add enough of the remaining flour so that the dough comes together. Knead by hand on a lightly floured board for one minute or until the dough is no longer sticky.

If you have a small food processor, process the dough in two batches and do not overwork dough.

THE NEXT STEP

PLACE THE DOUGH in a lightly oiled bowl and turn dough over so that it is very thinly coated all over with oil. Put the bowl in a large plastic bag and leave in a warm place until the dough has doubled in size. PUNCH DOWN and knead for 10 seconds so that the dough is back to its original size. Shape and let rise, covered with a dry cloth, until doubled in size. Bake in a preheated oven. (Refer to The Simplest, Speediest Way with Sweet Doughs page 106.)

This brown sugar dough rises more slowly than the one made with white sugar, but be patient. If you haven't killed the yeast with too much heat, trust me, your dough will rise eventually.

Sweet Orange Dough

30 g (1 oz) fresh yeast or
  1½ sachets dried yeast
¼ cup water, lukewarm for
  fresh yeast, warm for dried
1 cup orange juice at room
  temperature
2 teaspoons finely grated
  orange rind
1 level teaspoon salt
¾ cup sugar
2 level tablespoons melted
  butter or margarine
1 egg at room temperature,
  slightly beaten
3½ to 4 cups bread making
  flour or plain (all-purpose)
  flour sifted with 3 level
  teaspoons gluten flour

BY HAND

PLACE THE YEAST in a large mixing bowl, add the water and stir until the yeast dissolves. Add the orange juice, orange rind, salt, sugar, butter, egg and half of the flour and beat very well with a wooden spoon. Add almost all of the remaining flour, a half a cupful at a time. When the dough becomes too stiff for the spoon, use just one floured hand to knead the dough in the bowl.

TURN THE DOUGH onto a lightly floured board and knead for five minutes or until the dough no longer sticks to your hands or the board and it is smooth and elastic. Use just a very light sprinkling of flour on the board to stop the dough from sticking.

BY MIXER

PLACE THE YEAST and water in a large mixer bowl. Stir to dissolve yeast. Add the remaining ingredients and almost all of the flour and mix, using the dough hook and a low speed, until the dough comes together and leaves the sides and bottom of the bowl. Knead for three minutes, adding the extra flour if necessary. Knead by hand on a lightly floured board for one minute or until the dough is no longer sticky.

BY FOOD PROCESSOR

PLACE THE YEAST and water in the food processor bowl fitted with the steel blade. Pulse for 10 seconds to mix. Add the remaining ingredients and almost all of the flour and process, with several pulses to mix, for about one minute. Add enough of the remaining flour so that the dough comes together. Knead by hand on a lightly floured board for one minute or until the dough is no longer sticky. If you have a small food processor, process the dough in two batches and do not overwork dough.

THE NEXT STEP

PLACE THE DOUGH in a lightly oiled bowl and turn dough over so that it is very thinly coated all over with oil. Put the bowl in a large plastic bag and leave in a warm place until the dough has doubled in size. PUNCH DOWN and knead for 10 seconds so that the dough is back to its original size. Shape and let rise, covered with a dry cloth, until doubled in size. Bake in a preheated oven. (Refer to The Simplest, Speediest Way with Sweet Doughs, page 106.)

To give this dough an even stronger orange flavour cut the sugar quantity by half and add a tablespoon of orange marmalade or even orange liqueur.

Wholemeal Sweet Dough

30 g (1 oz) fresh yeast or 1½
   sachets dried yeast
¼ cup water, lukewarm for
   fresh yeast, warm for dried
   yeast
1 cup milk, lukewarm for
   fresh yeast, warm for dried
   yeast
1 level teaspoon salt
2 tablespoons light honey or
3 level tablespoons brown
   sugar
¼ cup oil or melted butter
1 egg, at room temperature,
   lightly beaten
2 cups wholemeal (whole-
   wheat) flour
1½ to 2 cups bread making
   flour or plain (all-purpose)
   flour sifted with 1 level
   teaspoon gluten flour

BY HAND

PLACE THE YEAST in a large mixing bowl, add the water and stir until the yeast dissolves. Add the milk, salt, honey, oil, egg and wholemeal flour and beat very well with a wooden spoon. Add almost all of the bread making flour, a half a cupful at a time. When the dough becomes too stiff for the spoon, use just one floured hand to knead the dough in the bowl.

TURN THE DOUGH onto a lightly floured board and knead for five minutes or until the dough no longer sticks to your hands or the board and it is smooth and elastic. Use just a very light sprinkling of flour on the board to stop the dough from sticking.

BY MIXER

PLACE THE YEAST and water in a large mixer bowl. Stir to dissolve yeast. Add the remaining ingredients and almost all of the bread making flour and mix, using the dough hook on low speed, until the dough comes together and leaves the sides and bottom of the bowl. Knead for three minutes, adding extra flour if necessary. Knead by hand for one minute or until dough is no longer sticky.

BY FOOD PROCESSOR

PLACE THE YEAST and water in the food processor bowl fitted with the steel blade. Pulse for 10 seconds to mix. Add the remaining ingredients and almost all of the bread making flour and process, with several pulses to mix, for about one minute. Add enough of the remaining flour so that the dough comes together. Knead by hand on a lightly floured board for one minute or until the dough is no longer sticky.

If you have a small food processor, process the dough in two batches and do not overwork dough.

THE NEXT STEP

PLACE THE DOUGH in a lightly oiled bowl and turn dough over so that it is very thinly coated all over with oil. Put the bowl in a large plastic bag and leave in a warm place until the dough has doubled in size.

PUNCH DOWN and knead for 10 seconds so that the dough is back to its original size. Shape and use any way you want to. (Refer to The Simplest, Speediest Way with Sweet Doughs, page 106.)

If you want to, you can use all wholemeal flour, but you get a much lighter result with the mix of wholemeal and plain (all-purpose) flours.

Sour Cream Dough

30 g (1 oz) fresh yeast or 1½ sachets dried yeast

¼ cup water, lukewarm for fresh yeast, warm for dried yeast

¾ cup sour cream at room temperature

1 level teaspoon salt

2 level tablespoons sugar

1 egg at room temperature, slightly beaten

3½ to 4 cups bread making flour or plain (all-purpose) flour sifted with 3 level teaspoons gluten flour

BY HAND

PLACE THE YEAST in a large mixing bowl, add the water and stir until the yeast dissolves. Add the sour cream, salt, sugar, egg and half of the flour and beat very well with a wooden spoon. Add almost all of the remaining flour, a half a cupful at a time. When the dough becomes too stiff for the spoon, use just one floured hand to knead the dough in the bowl.

TURN THE DOUGH onto a lightly floured board and knead for five minutes or until the dough no longer sticks to your hands or the board and it is smooth and elastic. Use just a very light sprinkling of flour on the board to stop the dough from sticking.

BY MIXER

PLACE THE YEAST and water in a large mixer bowl. Stir to dissolve yeast. Add the remaining ingredients and almost all of the flour and mix, using the dough hook and a low speed, until the dough comes together and leaves the sides and bottom of the bowl. Knead for three minutes, adding the extra flour if necessary. Knead by hand on a lightly floured board for one minute or until the dough is no longer sticky.

BY FOOD PROCESSOR

PLACE THE YEAST and water in the food processor bowl fitted with the steel blade. Pulse for 10 seconds to mix. Add the remaining ingredients and almost all of the flour and process, with several pulses to mix, for about one minute. Add enough of the remaining flour so that the dough comes together. Knead by hand on a lightly floured board for one minute or until the dough is no longer sticky.

If you have a small food processor, process the dough in two batches and do not overwork dough.

THE NEXT STEP

PLACE THE DOUGH in a lightly oiled bowl and turn dough over so that it is very thinly coated all over with oil. Put the bowl in a large plastic bag and leave in a warm place until the dough has doubled in size.
PUNCH DOWN and knead for 10 seconds so that the dough is back to its original size. Shape and let rise, covered with a dry cloth, until doubled in size. Bake in a preheated oven. (Refer to The Simplest, Speediest Way with Sweet Doughs, below.)
If you don't remember to take the sour cream from the refrigerator before making this dough, warm it just a little in the microwave oven or stand the container in a bowl of warm water to take the chill off it.

The Simplest Speediest Way with Sweet Doughs

When you are in a great hurry, just place the risen dough on a greased baking tray, spread with soft butter and speedily scatter or spread on a topping. Then cover with a cloth, let it rise again and bake in a preheated moderate oven (180°C/350°F) for about 25 to 30 minutes or until the underside is cooked.

Ten simple sweet fillings
(or use these as toppings)

Just mix the ingredients together.

(i)	(ii)
brown sugar	*½ cup soft butter*
cinnamon	*½ cup light honey*
sultanas (golden raisins)	*½ cup sugar*
	1 level teaspoon ground cinnamon

(iii)
1 cup cooked apples
¼ cup seedless raisins
¼ cup brown sugar
¼ cup chopped nuts
½ level teaspoon ground cinnamon
$^1/_8$ level teaspoon ground nutmeg

(iv)
½ cup raspberry jam
½ cup chopped glacé (candied) fruit
¼ cup seedless raisins
¼ cup chopped nuts

(v)
¼ cup soft butter
$^1/_3$ cup sugar
$^1/_3$ cup coconut
¼ cup chopped nuts
¼ level teaspoon ground cinnamon
1 tablespoon cream or milk
1 teaspoon pure vanilla essence

(vi)
½ cup brown sugar
2 level teaspoons ground cinnamon
2 level tablespoons chopped nuts
¾ cup sultanas (golden raisins)

(vii)
2 tablespoons soft butter
1½ cups coconut
½ cup golden syrup
   (light corn syrup)
1 cup chopped dates
rind and juice of 1 lemon

(viii)
2 tablespoons soft butter
2 level tablespoons brown sugar
2 level tablespoons rolled oats
½ teaspoon pure vanilla essence

(ix)
¼ cup soft butter
$^1/_3$ cup brown sugar
¾ cup raisins
$^1/_3$ cup chopped walnuts

(x)
¾ cup soft butter
½ cup brown sugar
3 tablespoons orange juice
¾ cup coconut

More Fanciful and Amusing Ways of Shaping Sweet Doughs

Bubble Ring

1 quantity of risen sweet
   dough
melted butter
brown sugar
chopped nuts

PINCH OFF walnut sized pieces of the risen dough and shape into balls. Dip in melted butter and roll in brown sugar. Place in layers in a very well greased 25 cm (10 in) springform pan, sprinkling on the nuts as you layer. Cover with a dry cloth and allow to rise until doubled in size.
PREHEAT OVEN to moderate (180°C/350°F).
BAKE FOR 35 to 40 minutes. Cool in the pan for five minutes before removing the sides of pan. Cool on a wire rack.

Daisy Cake

½ quantity of risen sweet
    dough
melted butter
sugar and cinnamon, mixed
    together

DIVIDE THE DOUGH into 12 pieces. Roll, pull and shape each piece into 15 cm (6 in) strips. Dip the strips into melted butter and then into the mixed sugar and cinnamon. Shape one strip into a coil and place on a well greased baking tray to make the centre of the daisy. Loop the remaining strips into petal shapes around the centre. Cover with a dry cloth and leave to rise until doubled in size.
PREHEAT OVEN to moderate (180°C/350°F).
BAKE FOR 25 to 30 minutes or until golden brown and there is no stale beer smell. Cool on a wire rack.

Snow Ring

1 quantity of risen sweet
    dough
soft butter
1 quantity of any filling

GLAZE
1 egg yolk beaten with 1
tablespoon water

ICING (FROSTING)
icing (confectioner's) sugar

DIVIDE THE risen dough into three equal parts. Roll and shape each portion into a flattened 50 cm (20 in) strip. Spread first with the soft butter and then with a little filling. Seal the filling in the dough by pushing the edges together. Plait (braid) the strips into a braid and join the ends together to make a ring shape. Place on a greased baking tray, cover with a dry cloth and allow to rise until doubled in size.
PREHEAT OVEN to moderate (180°C/350°F).
BRUSH WITH egg glaze and bake for 30 to 35 minutes or until the bottom is browned and there is no stale beer smell. Lift off the tray and cool on a wire rack. Dust thickly with icing sugar.

Topsy Turvy

1 quantity of risen sweet
    dough
soft butter
a double quantity of any filling

GLAZE
milk

ICING (FROSTING)
1 cup sifted icing
    (confectioner's) sugar
    blended with 1 to 2
    tablespoons milk (flavour
    or colour if desired)

ROLL THE RISEN dough into a 50 x 30 cm (20 x 12 in) rectangle and spread first with the soft butter and then with the filling. Roll up like a Swiss (jelly) roll, beginning at one of the long sides.
CUT INTO 5 cm (2 in) slices and arrange cut side down in a well greased 22 cm (9 in) ring tin. Cover with a dry cloth and allow to rise until doubled in size.
PREHEAT OVEN to moderate (180°C/350°F).
BRUSH LIGHTLY with a little milk. Bake for 35 to 40 minutes or until the bottom is browned and there is no stale beer smell. Turn onto a wire rack to cool and, when nearly cold, spread on the icing.

RIGHT: Kulich (page 122)

Twisty

1 quantity of risen sweet
  dough
soft butter
1 quantity of any filling

GLAZE
MILK

ICING (FROSTING)
1 cup sifted icing
  (confectioner's) sugar
  blended with 1 to 2
  tablespoons milk (flavour
  or colour if desired)

DIVIDE THE DOUGH into halves and roll one half into a 30 x 25 cm (12 x 10 in) rectangle. Spread first with the soft butter and then with half of the filling. Roll up like a Swiss (jelly) roll beginning at one of the long sides. Pinch the edge to seal. Repeat with the other half of the dough.

PLACE BOTH ROLLS, seam side down and 5 cm (2 in) apart, on a well greased baking tray. With scissors or a sharp knife, cut deep into each roll at 2.5 cm (1 in) intervals. Do not cut completely through the rolls of dough.

FOLD ALTERNATING slices, right and left, and turn each slice on its sides so that the slices overlap in the centre to make one cake. Cover with a dry cloth and allow to rise until doubled in size. Preheat oven to moderate (180°C/350°F).

BRUSH LIGHTLY with a little milk. Bake for 25 to 30 minutes or until the bottom is browned and there is no stale beer smell. Turn onto a wire rack to cool and, when nearly cold, spread on the icing.

Roundabout

1 quantity of risen sweet
  dough
soft butter
a double quantity of any
  filling

GLAZE
milk

ICING (FROSTING)
1 cup sifted icing
  (confectioner's) sugar
  blended with 1 to 2
  tablespoons milk (flavour
  or colour if desired)

ROLL THE RISEN dough into a 35 x 30 cm (14 x 12 in) rectangle. Spread first with soft butter and then with the filling. Roll up like a Swiss (jelly) roll beginning at one of the long sides. Pinch the edge to seal and join the ends to make a ring. With scissors or a sharp knife, cut halfway through the roll all the way around the circle to expose the filling. Cover with a dry cloth and allow to rise until doubled in size.

PREHEAT OVEN to moderate (180°C/350°F).

BRUSH LIGHTLY with milk. Bake for 25 to 30 minutes or until the bottom is browned and there is no stale beer smell. Turn onto a wire rack to cool and, when nearly cold, spread on the icing.

LEFT: *Dark Rye Bread (page 35)*

Crisscross

1 quantity of risen sweet
  dough
soft butter
a double quantity of any
  filling

GLAZE
milk

ICING (FROSTING)
1 cup sifted icing
  (confectioner's) sugar
  blended with 1 to 2
  tablespoons milk
  (flavour or
  colour if desired)

ROLL OUT the risen dough into a 40 cm (16 in) square. Place on a well greased baking tray and spread with soft butter. Spread the filling down the centre of the dough. Cut the dough diagonally at 2.5 cm (1 in) intervals on both sides. Fold alternate strips of dough over the filling, crossing in the centre. Cover with a dry cloth and allow to rise until doubled in size again.

PREHEAT OVEN to moderate (180°C/350°F).

BRUSH LIGHTLY with a little milk. Bake for 35 to 40 minutes or until the bottom is browned and there is no stale beer smell. Turn onto a wire rack to cool and, when nearly cold, spread on the icing.

Tea Ring

1 quantity of risen sweet
  dough
soft butter
a double quantity of any
  filling

GLAZE
milk

ICING (FROSTING)
1 cup sifted icing
  (confectioner's) sugar
  blended with 1 to 2
  tablespoons milk (flavour
  or colour if desired)

ROLL OUT the risen dough into a 54 x 30 cm (22 x 12 in) rectangle. Spread with soft butter and then the filling. Roll up like a Swiss (jelly) roll beginning at one of the long sides. Pinch the edge to seal. Shape into a ring, join the ends and place on a greased baking tray.

WITH SCISSORS or a sharp knife make deep cuts into the ring 2.5 cm (1 in) apart. With your fingers, push each slice in turn, one to the centre and one to the outside, and so on all the way around. Cover with a dry cloth and leave to rise until doubled in size.

PREHEAT OVEN to moderate (180°C/350°F).

BRUSH LIGHTLY with milk and bake for 30 to 35 minutes or until the bottom is browned and there is no stale beer smell. Cool on a wire rack and, when nearly cold, spread on the icing.

Icings (Frostings)

Icings give a finishing touch to your cakes. Pick a flavour that you think goes well with your cake and then drizzle or spread it on. I have found the easiest way to get icing onto a cake is to make it in a paper cup. I then squeeze the edge to make a pouring lip and I can then pour the icing where I want it to go, not where it wants to go. Ice the cakes while they are still warm, never hot, and then you can sprinkle with nuts before the icing sets.

The Basic Icing (Frosting)

*1 cup sifted icing
(confectioner's) sugar
1 to 2 tablespoons milk*

Mix both ingredients together and blend until smooth. If the mixture is too thin, add more icing sugar. Some variations are:

- Vanilla
  Add ½ teaspoon pure vanilla essence.

- Almond
  Add ¼ teaspoon almond essence.

- Strawberry
  Add ½ teaspoon strawberry essence and a few drops of pink colouring.

- Lemon
  Add ¼ teaspoon grated lemon rind and substitute lemon juice for the milk.

- Orange
  Add ¼ teaspoon grated orange rind and substitute orange juice for milk.

- Chocolate
  Add 1 level tablespoon cocoa.

- Coffee
  Add ½ level teaspoon instant coffee.

- Mocha
  Add 1 level tablespoon cocoa and ½ level teaspoon instant coffee.

- Spice
  Add ¼ level teaspoon ground cinnamon and a dash of ground nutmeg.

- Rum
  Add ¼ teaspoon rum essence or 1 teaspoon real rum.

Chelsea Buns

20 g (¾ oz) fresh yeast or
  1 sachet dried yeast
½ cup water, lukewarm for
  fresh yeast, warm for dried
  yeast
¾ cup milk, lukewarm for
  fresh yeast, warm for dried
  yeast
1 level teaspoon salt
⅓ cup sugar
⅓ cup melted butter or
  margarine
1 egg at room temperature,
  slightly beaten
grated rind of 1 lemon
1 level teaspoon ground
  cinnamon
3½ to 4 cups bread making
  flour or plain (all-purpose)
  flour sifted with 3 level
  teaspoons gluten flour
extra sugar

THE FILLING
⅓ cup soft butter
½ cup brown sugar
½ cup sultanas (golden
  raisins)
½ cup currants

GLAZE
1 tablespoon of sugar
¼ cup milk

BY HAND

PLACE THE YEAST in a large mixing bowl, add the water and stir until the yeast dissolves. Add the milk, salt, sugar, melted butter, eggs, lemon rind, cinnamon and half of the flour and beat very well with a wooden spoon. Add almost all of the remaining flour, a half a cupful at a time. When the dough becomes too stiff for the spoon, use just one floured hand to knead the dough in the bowl. TURN THE DOUGH onto a lightly floured board and knead for five minutes or until the dough no longer sticks to your hands or the board and it is smooth and elastic. Use just a very light sprinkling of flour on the board to stop the dough from sticking.

BY MIXER

PLACE THE YEAST and water in a large mixer bowl. Stir to dissolve the yeast. Add the remaining ingredients and almost all of the flour and mix, using the dough hook and a low speed, until the dough comes together and leaves the sides and bottom of the bowl. Knead for three minutes, adding the extra flour if necessary. Knead by hand on a lightly floured board for one minute or until the dough is no longer sticky.

BY FOOD PROCESSOR

PLACE THE YEAST and water in the food processor bowl fitted with the steel blade. Pulse for 10 seconds to mix. Add the remaining ingredients and almost all of the flour and process, with several pulses to mix, for about one minute. Add enough of the remaining flour so that the dough comes together. Knead by hand on a lightly floured board for one minute or until the dough is no longer sticky.

If you have a small food processor, process the dough in two batches and do not overwork dough.

THE NEXT STEP

PLACE THE DOUGH in a lightly oiled bowl and turn dough over so that it is very thinly coated all over with oil. Put the bowl in a large plastic bag and leave in a warm place until the dough has doubled in size.

PUNCH DOWN and knead for 10 seconds so that the dough is back to its original size.

ROLL OUT into a large rectangle and spread with the filling. Roll up tightly like a Swiss (jelly) roll and cut into slices 4 cm (1½ in) thick. Place cut side down, 2.5 cm (1 in) apart, on a greased baking tray, leaving room for the slices to spread. Sprinkle lightly with

the extra sugar and cover with a dry cloth. .
doubled in size.
PREHEAT OVEN to moderately hot (200°C/400°F).
BAKE FOR 15 to 20 minutes or until the bottoms are b.
there is no stale beer smell.
PREPARE THE GLAZE by heating the sugar and milk in a small
pan. Brush the buns with the glaze.

Hot Cross Buns

An English bread for Good Friday

*20 g (¾ oz) fresh yeast or
1 sachet dried yeast*
*¼ cup water, lukewarm for
fresh yeast, warm for dried
yeast*
*¾ cup milk, lukewarm for fresh
yeast, warm for dried yeast*
1 level teaspoon salt
¼ cup sugar
¼ cup melted butter
*1 egg at room temperature,
lightly beaten*
*1 level teaspoon mixed spice
or ½ level teaspoon ground
cinnamon, ¼ level teaspoon
ground nutmeg and ¼
level teaspoon ground cloves)*
*½ cup sultanas (golden
raisins)*
*¼ cup chopped mixed
(candied) peel*
*3½ to 4 cups bread making
flour or plain (all-purpose)
flour sifted with 3 level
teaspoons gluten flour*

BATTER FOR CROSSES
*½ cup plain (all-purpose)
flour*
4 tablespoons water

FINISHING GLAZE
1 level tablespoon sugar
1 level tablespoon water
1 level teaspoon gelatine

BY HAND

PLACE THE YEAST in a large mixing bowl, add the water and stir
until the yeast dissolves. Add the milk, salt, sugar, butter, egg, spices,
and half of the flour and beat very well with a wooden spoon. Add
almost all of the remaining flour, a half a cupful at a time. When the
dough becomes too stiff for the spoon, use just one floured hand
to knead the dough in the bowl.
TURN THE DOUGH onto a lightly floured board and knead for five
minutes or until the dough no longer sticks to your hands or the
board and it is smooth and elastic. Use just a very light sprinkling
of flour on the board to stop the dough from sticking.

BY MIXER

PLACE THE YEAST and water in a large mixer bowl. Stir to dissolve
yeast. Add the milk, salt, sugar, butter, egg, spices, and almost all of
the flour and mix, using the dough hook and a low speed, until
the dough comes together and leaves the sides and bottom of the
bowl. Knead for three minutes, adding the extra flour if necessary.
Knead by hand on a lightly floured board for one minute or until
the dough is no longer sticky.

BY FOOD PROCESSOR

PLACE THE YEAST and water in the food processor bowl fitted with
the steel blade. Pulse for 10 seconds to mix. Add the milk, salt,
sugar, butter, egg, spices, and almost all of the flour and process,
with several pulses to mix, for about one minute. Add enough of
the remaining flour so that the dough comes together. Knead on a
lightly floured board for one minute or until the dough is no longer
sticky.

If you have a small food processor, process the dough in two
batches and do not overwork dough.

THE NEXT STEP

PLACE THE DOUGH in a lightly oiled bowl and turn dough over so that it is very thinly coated all over with oil. Put the bowl in a large plastic bag and leave in a warm place until the dough has doubled in size.

PUNCH DOWN and knead for 10 seconds so that the dough is back to its original size. Knead in the sultanas and mixed peel. Divide the dough into 16 even sized pieces and shape each piece into a round. Place on a greased baking tray and leave 1.25 cm (½ in) between the buns. Cover with a dry cloth and leave to rise until doubled in size again.

PREPARE THE BATTER by mixing the flour and water together to make a very soft paste. If you do not have a piping bag, place the batter in a small strong plastic bag or envelope and snip off one corner to make a small hole. Pipe batter crosses on each bun. Preheat oven to hot (220°C/425°F).

BAKE FOR 15 to 20 minutes or until there is no stale beer smell.

TO PREPARE the finishing glaze, place all ingredients in a small saucepan and stir over a low heat until dissolved.

Lift the buns off the tray and place on a wire rack. While still hot brush with the glaze.

If you want to bake these on Good Friday, prepare the dough the night before. Refrigerate it (it will rise even if it is cold) and in the morning punch down the dough, shape, let rise in a warm kitchen and then bake. The smell of freshly baked buns is a wonderful start to a happy Easter.

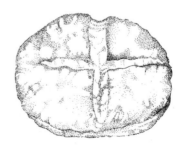

Panettone

An Italian bread for Christmas

30 g (1 oz) fresh yeast or
1½ sachets dried yeast
²/₃ cup milk, lukewarm for
fresh yeast, warm for dried
yeast
pinch of salt
¼ cup sugar
2 teaspoons honey
¼ cup melted unsalted
butter
1 teaspoon vanilla
3 large egg yolks
grated rind of half a lemon
grated rind of half an orange
3½ to 4 cups bread
making flour or plain (all-
purpose) flour sifted with 3
level teaspoons gluten flour
½ cup mixed peel (candied
orange and lemon)
½ cup raisins

GLAZE
extra melted butter

BY HAND

PLACE THE YEAST in a large mixing bowl, add the milk and stir until the yeast dissolves. Add the salt, sugar, honey, butter, vanilla, egg yolks, grated rinds and half the flour and beat very well with a wooden spoon. Add almost all of the remaining flour, a half a cupful at a time. When the dough becomes too stiff for the spoon, use just one floured hand to knead the dough in the bowl.

TURN THE DOUGH onto a lightly floured board and knead for five minutes or until the dough no longer sticks to your hands or the board and it is smooth and elastic. Use just a very light sprinkling of flour on the board to stop the dough from sticking.

BY MIXER

PLACE THE YEAST and milk in a large mixer bowl. Stir to dissolve yeast. Add the salt, sugar, honey, butter, vanilla, egg yolks, grated rinds and almost all of the flour and mix, using the dough hook and a low speed, until the dough comes together and leaves the sides and bottom of the bowl. Knead for three minutes, adding the extra flour if necessary. Knead by hand on a lightly floured board for one minute or until the dough is no longer sticky.

BY FOOD PROCESSOR

PLACE THE YEAST and milk in the food processor bowl fitted with the steel blade. Pulse for 10 seconds to mix. Add the salt, sugar, honey, butter, vanilla, egg yolks, grated rinds and almost all of the flour and process, with several pulses to mix, for about one minute. Add enough of the remaining flour so that the dough comes together.

If you only have a small food processor, process the dough in two batches and do not overwork dough.

THE NEXT STEP

PLACE THE DOUGH in a lightly oiled bowl and turn dough over so that it is thinly coated all over with oil. Put the bowl in a large plastic bag and leave in a warm place until the dough has doubled in size.

PUNCH DOWN and knead in the peel and raisins. Shape into a round and place in a deep well greased 15 cm (6 in) round cake pan (or use a camping billy can) with a round of baking parchment on the bottom. Cut a cross in the top of the loaf with a very sharp thin knife or a single edged razor blade. Cover with a dry cloth and leave to rise until doubled in size again.

PREHEAT OVEN to moderately hot (200°C/400°F).
BRUSH THE TOP with some of the glaze and bake for 10 minutes.
BRUSH LIGHTLY with more glaze and reduce the oven heat to moderate (180°C/350°F). Bake for a further 45 minutes or until a thin skewer inserted in the centre comes out clean. Leave in the pan for five minutes before turning the loaf onto a wire rack to cool on its side.

All the Italians I know insist that Christmas is not really right if this celebration bread is missing. It's traditionally meant to be eaten just at Christmas, and preferably with sinfully rich mascarpone, but it's to be found in the shops many weeks and even months before then.

Colomba Di Pasqua
An Italian dove-shaped bread for Easter

30 g (1 oz) fresh yeast or
  1½ sachets dried yeast
¼ cup water, lukewarm for
  fresh yeast, warm for dried
  yeast
½ cup milk, lukewarm for
  fresh yeast, warm for dried
  yeast
½ level teaspoon salt
⅓ cup sugar
½ cup soft unsalted butter
4 egg yolks at room
  temperature
2 teaspoons pure vanilla
1 teaspoon finely grated
  lemon rind
3½ to 4 cups bread making
  flour or plain (all-purpose)
  flour sifted with 2 level
  teaspoons gluten flour

ALMOND PASTE TOPPING
1 egg white
⅓ cup prepared marzipan

GLAZE AND DECORATION
egg white beaten with a
  little water
2 level teaspoons extra sugar
¼ cup slivered almonds

BY HAND
PLACE THE YEAST in a large mixing bowl, add the water and stir until the yeast dissolves. Add the milk, salt, sugar, butter, egg yolks, vanilla essence, lemon rind and half of the flour and beat very well with a wooden spoon. Add almost all of the remaining flour, a half a cupful at a time. When the dough becomes too stiff for the spoon, use just one floured hand to knead the dough in the bowl.
TURN THE DOUGH onto a lightly floured board and knead for five minutes or until the dough no longer sticks to your hands or the board and it is smooth and elastic. Use just a very light sprinkling of flour on the board to stop the dough from sticking.

BY MIXER
PLACE THE YEAST and water in a large mixer bowl. Stir to dissolve yeast. Add the remaining ingredients and almost all of the flour and mix, using the dough hook and a low speed, until the dough comes together and leaves the sides and bottom of the bowl. Knead for three minutes, adding the extra flour if necessary. Knead by hand on a lightly floured board for one minute or until the dough is no longer sticky.

BY FOOD PROCESSOR
PLACE THE YEAST and water in the food processor bowl fitted with the steel blade. Pulse for 10 seconds to mix. Add the remaining ingredients and almost all of the flour and process, with several pulses to mix, for about one minute. Add enough of the remaining flour so that the dough comes together. Knead by hand on a lightly floured board for one minute or until the dough is no longer sticky.

If you have a small food processor, process the dough in two batches and do not overwork dough.

THE NEXT STEP

PLACE THE DOUGH in a lightly oiled bowl and turn dough over so that it is very thinly coated all over with oil. Put the bowl in a large plastic bag and leave in a warm place until the dough has doubled in size. Punch down and knead for 30 seconds so that the dough is back to its original size.

TO SHAPE the dove, divide the dough in half. Roll one piece into a large oval about 15 x 30 cm (6 x 12 in) to make the two wings. For the head and body, roll the second piece into a long narrow triangle about 30 cm (12 in) long and 15 cm (6 in) at the base. Place across over the wings and, holding the triangle in the centre, twist it over once and flatten the base to make the tail. With your fingers, pull out a beak at the top of the triangle. Use a very thin sharp knife or a single edged razor blade to shape the tail feathers. Prepare the Almond Paste topping by blending the ingredients together to make a smooth paste. Spread the almond paste topping over the wings and tail. Cover with a dry cloth and let rise until nearly doubled in size.

PREHEAT OVEN to moderately slow (160°C/325°F).

BRUSH WITH egg white glaze and sprinkle wings and tail with extra sugar and slivered almonds.

BAKE FOR 45 to 50 minutes or until browned and there is no stale beer smell. Cool on a wire rack.

I've had students in classes making this bird with some of them doing it perfectly and others ending up with wonderfully weird shapes that didn't look like doves at all. But, we all enjoyed the laughter such breads gave us much more than the admiration demanded for the perfect ones.

Christopsomo

A Greek bread for Christmas

*30 g (1 oz) fresh yeast or
1½ sachets dried yeast
¼ cup water, lukewarm for
fresh yeast, warm for dried
yeast
¼ cup milk, lukewarm for
fresh yeast, warm for dried
yeast
½ level teaspoon salt
¼ cup sugar
½ cup soft butter
2 eggs at room temperature,
lightly beaten
1 teaspoon anise seeds,
crushed
3½ to 4 cups bread making
flour or plain (all-purpose)
flour sifted with 3 level
teaspoons gluten flour*

GLAZE AND DECORATION
*9 walnut halves or 9 glacé
(candied) cherries
beaten egg mixed with a
little water*

BY HAND

PLACE THE YEAST in a large mixing bowl, add the water and stir until the yeast dissolves. Add the milk, salt, sugar, butter, eggs, spice and half of the flour and beat very well with a wooden spoon. Add almost all of the remaining flour, a half a cupful at a time. When the dough becomes too stiff for the spoon, use just one floured hand to knead the dough in the bowl.

TURN THE DOUGH onto a lightly floured board and knead for five minutes or until the dough no longer sticks to your hands or the board and it is smooth and elastic. Use just a very light sprinkling of flour on the board to stop the dough from sticking.

BY MIXER

PLACE THE YEAST and water in a large mixer bowl. Stir to dissolve yeast. Add the remaining ingredients and almost all of the flour and mix, using the dough hook and a low speed, until the dough comes together and leaves the sides and bottom of the bowl. Knead for three minutes, adding the extra flour if necessary. Knead by hand on a lightly floured board for one minute or until the dough is no longer sticky.

BY FOOD PROCESSOR

PLACE THE YEAST and water in the food processor bowl fitted with the steel blade. Pulse for 10 seconds to mix. Add the remaining ingredients and almost all of the flour and process, with several pulses to mix, for about one minute. Add enough of the remaining flour so that the dough comes together. Knead by hand on a lightly floured board for one minute or until the dough is no longer sticky.

If you have a small food processor, process the dough in two batches and do not overwork dough.

THE NEXT STEP

PLACE THE DOUGH in a lightly oiled bowl and turn dough over so that it is very thinly coated all over with oil. Put the bowl in a large plastic bag and leave in a warm place until the dough has doubled in size.

PUNCH DOWN and knead for 10 seconds so that the dough is back to its original size. Cut off two-thirds of the dough and shape into a round. Place on a greased baking tray.

DIVIDE THE remaining dough in half and shape, stretch and roll each half into a 30 cm (12 in) long strand. Cut a 10 cm (4 in) slash into each end of the two strands and gently place strands across the centre of the round, on the tray, to form a cross. Curl the slashed edges outwards to form a circle.

PLACE THE walnuts in the centre of each curl, retaining just one walnut half. Place that remaining walnut half in the centre of the cross. Brush with beaten egg glaze, cover and let rise again until doubled in size again.

PREHEAT OVEN to moderate (180°C/350°F).

BAKE FOR 40 to 45 minutes or until a skewer inserted in the centre comes out clean. Cool on a wire rack.

A Greek friend tells me she still remembers her grandmother making this bread and the delight they all felt when she started her baking as it meant Christmas was not too far away.

Lambropsomo

A Greek bread for Easter

20 g (¾ oz) fresh yeast or
  1 sachet dried yeast
½ cup milk, lukewarm for
  fresh yeast, warm for dried
  yeast
½ level teaspoon salt
½ cup caster sugar
½ cup soft butter
2 eggs at room temperature,
  lightly beaten
1 level teaspoon finely grated
  lemon rind
3½ to 4 cups bread making
  flour or plain (all-purpose)
  flour sifted with 3 level
  teaspoons gluten flour

GLAZE AND DECORATION
6 or more hard cooked eggs
  dyed scarlet (one for each
  person)
beaten egg mixed with a
  little water
sesame seeds

BY HAND

PLACE THE YEAST in a large mixing bowl, add the milk and stir until the yeast dissolves. Add the salt, sugar, butter, eggs, lemon rind and half of the flour and beat very well with a wooden spoon. Add almost all of the remaining flour, a half a cupful at a time. When the dough becomes too stiff for the spoon, use just one floured hand to knead the dough in the bowl.

TURN THE DOUGH onto a lightly floured board and knead for five minutes or until the dough no longer sticks to your hands or the board and it is smooth and elastic. Use just a very light sprinkling of flour on the board to stop the dough from sticking.

BY MIXER

PLACE THE YEAST and milk in a large mixer bowl. Stir to dissolve yeast. Add the remaining ingredients and almost all of the flour and mix, using the dough hook and a low speed, until the dough comes together and leaves the sides and bottom of the bowl. Knead for three minutes, adding the extra flour if necessary. Knead by hand on a lightly floured board for one minute or until the dough is no longer sticky.

BY FOOD PROCESSOR

PLACE THE YEAST and milk in the food processor bowl fitted with the steel blade. Pulse for 10 seconds to mix. Add the remaining ingredients and almost all of the flour and process, with several pulses to mix, for about one minute. Add enough of the remaining flour so that the dough comes together. Knead by hand on a lightly floured board for one minute or until the dough is no longer sticky.

If you have a small food processor, process the dough in two batches and do not overwork dough.

THE NEXT STEP

PLACE THE DOUGH in a lightly oiled bowl and turn dough over so that it is very thinly coated all over with oil. Put the bowl in a large plastic bag and leave in a warm place until the dough has doubled in size.

PUNCH DOWN and knead for 10 seconds so that the dough is back to its original size. Divide the dough into three equal pieces and roll and shape each piece into a strand 50 cm (20 in) long. Place strands alongside each other on a greased baking tray and plait (braid).

PINCH THE ENDS of the strands together to seal. Tuck the dyed hard cooked eggs into the loaf. Cover with a dry cloth and leave to rise until nearly doubled in size again.

PREHEAT OVEN to moderate (180°C/350°F).

BRUSH WITH beaten egg glaze and sprinkle with sesame seeds. Bake for 30 to 35 minutes or until loaf sounds hollow when tapped on the bottom. Cool on a wire rack.

The Greek way to go with the coloured eggs is for everyone to try to smash the eggs of the others with their own egg. The person with the intact egg, after all others are shattered, is 'The Winner'!

Kugelhupf

A middle-European cake for birthdays

20 g (¾ oz) fresh yeast or
  1 sachet dried yeast
¼ cup water, lukewarm for
  fresh yeast, warm for dried
  yeast
½ cup milk, lukewarm for
  fresh yeast, warm for dried
  yeast
½ level teaspoon salt
½ cup sugar
½ cup soft unsalted butter
3 eggs at room temperature,
  lightly beaten
finely grated peel of 1 lemon
2¾ cups bread making
  flour or plain (all-purpose)
  flour sifted with 1 level
  teaspoon gluten flour
½ cup sultanas (golden
  raisins)

DECORATION
¹/₃ cup very finely chopped
  almonds
blanched almonds

BY HAND

PLACE THE YEAST in a large mixing bowl, add the water and stir until the yeast dissolves. Add the milk, salt, sugar, butter, eggs, lemon peel and half of the flour and beat very well with a wooden spoon. Add almost all of the remaining flour, a half a cupful at a time. Beat for five minutes.

BY MIXER

PLACE THE YEAST and water in a large mixer bowl. Stir to dissolve yeast. Add the remaining ingredients, except the sultanas, and half of the flour and mix at a medium speed for four minutes. Stir in the remaining flour and scrape batter from the sides of the bowl.

BY FOOD PROCESSOR

PLACE THE YEAST and water in the food processor bowl fitted with the steel blade. Pulse for 10 seconds to mix. Add the remaining ingredients, except the sultanas, and half of the flour. Process, with several pulses to mix, for about one minute. Knead by hand on a lightly floured board for one minute or until the dough is no longer sticky.

If you have a small food processor, process the dough in two batches and do not overwork dough.

THE NEXT STEP

PUT THE BOWL in a large plastic bag and leave in a warm place until the dough has doubled in size. Mix in the sultanas and stir with a spoon to punch down.

GREASE THE SIDES and bottom of a nine cup fluted or plain ring tin and sprinkle on the chopped almonds. Arrange the blanched almonds evenly in the bottom of the pan. Pour in the cake batter and cover with a dry cloth. Let rise until doubled in size again.

PREHEAT OVEN to moderate (180°C/350°F).

BAKE FOR 50 minutes or until a skewer inserted in the centre comes out clean. Leave in the pan for five minutes before turning onto a wire rack to cool.

I had a dear Austrian friend who thought it was wickedly extravagant to use chopped almonds in the greased tin and would use dried breadcrumbs instead. As much as I loved her, I think the almonds are nicer.

Kulich with Pashka

A Russian bread for Easter Sunday

30 g (1 oz) fresh yeast or
  1½ sachets dried yeast
½ cup milk, lukewarm for
  fresh yeast, warm for dried
  yeast
½ level teaspoon salt
½ cup sugar
½ cup soft unsalted butter
½ teaspoon pure vanilla
  essence
3 eggs at room temperature,
  lightly beaten
½ cup sultanas (golden
  raisins)
¼ cup glacé (candied)
cherries, chopped
2 tablespoons blanched
  almonds, coarsely chopped
2¾ cups bread making
  flour or plain (all-purpose)
  flour sifted with 1 level
  teaspoon gluten flour

GLAZE
beaten egg and water

WHITE ICING
1 cup icing (confectioners')
  sugar, sifted
1 tablespoon water or milk
½ teaspoon pure vanilla
  essence

You will need to make the Pashka first as it must be refrigerated for at least six hours.

BY HAND
PLACE THE YEAST in a large mixing bowl, add the milk and stir until the yeast dissolves. Add the salt, sugar, butter, vanilla essence, eggs, sultanas, glacé cherries, almonds and half of the flour and beat very well with a wooden spoon for five minutes.

BY MIXER
PLACE THE YEAST and milk in a large mixer bowl. Stir to dissolve yeast. Add the remaining ingredients and half of the flour and mix at a medium speed for four minutes. Stir in the remaining flour and scrape batter from the sides of the bowl.

BY FOOD PROCESSOR
PLACE THE YEAST and milk in the food processor bowl fitted with the steel blade. Pulse for 10 seconds to mix. Add half of the flour and process, with several pulses to mix, for about one minute. By hand, stir in the remaining flour and ingredients.

If you have a small food processor, process the dough in two batches and do not overwork dough.

THE NEXT STEP
PUT THE BOWL in a large plastic bag and leave in a warm place until the dough has doubled in size. Stir with a spoon to punch down.

GREASE THE SIDES and bottom of a eight cup billy can or fruit juice can and line the base with a circle of baking parchment. Pour in the cake batter and cover with a dry cloth. Let rise until doubled in size again.

PREHEAT OVEN to moderate (180°C/350°F).

BRUSH THE TOP with the egg glaze. Bake for 50 minutes or until a skewer inserted in the centre comes out clean. Leave in the pan for five minutes before turning onto a wire rack to cool.

WHITE ICING
PREPARE THE white icing by mixing all of the ingredients together until smooth.

PASHKA

250 g (8 oz) unsalted butter
1 cup caster sugar
1 cup sour cream
1 teaspoon pure vanilla
    essence
1 egg yolk
1 cup blanched almonds,
    coarsely chopped
1 cup mixed (candied) peel,
    chopped
1 cup seedless raisins,
    chopped
red, green and yellow glacé
    (candied) cherries for
    garnish
slivered almonds for garnish

PASHKA

LINE A TALL, sloping four sided six cup pashka mould or a tall six cup plastic container with cheesecloth. Beat the butter and sugar together until creamy. Mix in the sour cream, vanilla essence, egg yolk, almonds, mixed peel and the raisins. Pack into the lined mould and place a heavy weight on the top to compress the mixture. Refrigerate for at least six hours and then unmould onto a serving plate. Use the cherries and the almonds to make X.B. (for Christ is Risen) on two sides.

When the bread is nearly cold, drizzle icing over the top and let it trickle down the sides. Serve on Easter Sunday with creamy pashka.

Challah

A bread for the Jewish Sabbath

20 g (¾ oz) fresh yeast or
    1 sachet dried yeast
1 cup water, lukewarm for
    fresh yeast, warm for dried
    yeast
1 level tablespoon salt
2 level teaspoons sugar
2 tablespoons oil
3 eggs at room temperature,
    lightly beaten
3½ to 4 cups bread making
    flour or plain (all-purpose)
    flour sifted with 3 level
    teaspoons gluten flour

GLAZE
beaten egg with a little water

DECORATION
poppyseeds

BY HAND

PLACE THE YEAST in a large mixing bowl, add the water and stir until the yeast dissolves. Add the salt, sugar, oil, eggs and half of the flour and beat very well with a wooden spoon. Add almost all of the remaining flour, a half a cupful at a time. When the dough becomes too stiff for the spoon, use just one floured hand to knead the dough in the bowl.

TURN THE DOUGH onto a lightly floured board and knead for five minutes or until the dough no longer sticks to your hands or the board and it is smooth and elastic. Use just a very light sprinkling of flour on the board to stop the dough from sticking.

BY MIXER

PLACE THE YEAST and water in a large mixer bowl. Stir to dissolve yeast. Add the remaining ingredients and almost all of the flour and mix, using the dough hook and a low speed, until the dough comes together and leaves the sides and bottom of the bowl. Knead for three minutes, adding the extra flour if necessary. Knead by hand on a lightly floured board for one minute or until the dough is no longer sticky.

BY FOOD PROCESSOR

PLACE THE YEAST and water in the food processor bowl fitted with the steel blade. Pulse for 10 seconds to mix. Add the remaining ingredients and almost all of the flour and process, with several pulses to mix, for about one minute. Add enough of the remaining flour so that the dough comes together. Knead by hand on a lightly floured board for one minute or until the dough is no longer sticky. If you have a small food processor, process the dough in two batches and do not overwork dough.

THE NEXT STEP
PLACE THE DOUGH in a lightly oiled bowl and turn dough over so that it is very thinly coated all over with oil. Put the bowl in a large plastic bag and leave in a warm place until the dough has doubled in size.

PUNCH DOWN and knead for 10 seconds so that the dough is back to its original size. Divide the dough into four. Pull, stretch and roll three of the balls of dough into 25 cm (10 in) ropes. Place ropes alongside each other on a greased baking tray.

PLAIT (BRAID) THE STRANDS together. Divide the reserved ball of dough into three and roll into strands. Plait these strands together and place on top of the first plait. Brush with beaten egg glaze and sprinkle with poppyseeds. Cover with a dry cloth and let rise until nearly doubled in size again.

PREHEAT OVEN to moderately hot (200°C/400°F).

BAKE FOR 45 to 50 minutes or until the bread sounds hollow when tapped and there is no stale beer smell. Cool on a wire rack.

This bread is for the Jewish Sabbath and represents the manna (spiritual food) found in the wilderness just when it was really needed. It is often served covered with a white cloth that symbolises the early morning dew.

Barmbrack

An Irish bread for Halloween

30 g (1 oz) fresh yeast or
  1½ sachets dried yeast
¼ cup water, lukewarm for
  fresh yeast, warm for dried
  yeast
¾ cup milk, lukewarm for
  fresh yeast, warm for dried
  yeast
1 level teaspoon salt
½ cup sugar
¼ cup soft butter
1 level teaspoon ground
  nutmeg
3½ to 4 cups bread making
  flour or plain (all-purpose)
  flour sifted with 2 level
  teaspoons gluten flour
½ cup sultanas (golden
  raisins)
½ cup currants
½ cup mixed (candied)
  peel, chopped

SUGAR GLAZE
2 level tablespoons sugar
1 level tablespoon

BY HAND

PLACE THE YEAST in a large mixing bowl, add the water and stir until the yeast dissolves. Add the milk, salt, sugar, butter, nutmeg and half of the flour and beat very well with a wooden spoon. Add almost all of the remaining flour, a half a cupful at a time. When the dough becomes too stiff for the spoon, use just one floured hand to knead the dough in the bowl.

TURN THE DOUGH onto a lightly floured board and knead for five minutes or until the dough no longer sticks to your hands or the board and it is smooth and elastic. Use just a very light sprinkling of flour on the board to stop the dough from sticking.

BY MIXER

PLACE THE YEAST and water in a large mixer bowl. Stir to dissolve yeast. Add the remaining ingredients, except the dried fruit and peel, and almost all of the flour. Mix, using the dough hook and a low speed, until the dough comes together and leaves the sides and bottom of the bowl. Knead for three minutes, adding the extra flour if necessary. Knead by hand on a lightly floured board for one minute or until the dough is no longer sticky.

BY FOOD PROCESSOR

PLACE THE YEAST and water in the food processor bowl fitted with the steel blade. Pulse for 10 seconds to mix. Add the remaining ingredients, except the dried fruit and peel, and almost all of the flour. Process, with several pulses to mix, for about one minute. Add enough of the remaining flour so that the dough comes together. Knead by hand on a lightly floured board for one minute or until the dough is no longer sticky.

If you have a small food processor, process the dough in two batches and do not overwork dough.

THE NEXT STEP

PLACE THE DOUGH in a lightly oiled bowl and turn dough over so that it is very thinly coated all over with oil. Put the bowl in a large plastic bag and leave in a warm place until the dough has doubled in size.

PUNCH DOWN and knead for 10 seconds so that the dough is back to its original size. Knead in the fruit and peel. Shape into a round and place on a greased baking tray. Cover with a dry cloth and leave to rise until doubled in size again.

PREHEAT OVEN to moderate (180°C/350°F).

BAKE FOR 40 to 50 minutes or until the loaf sounds hollow when tapped on the bottom.

TO PREPARE the glaze, place the sugar and water in a small screwtop jar. Put on the lid and shake vigorously to mix.

Brush the bread with the sugar glaze and cool on a wire rack.

Stollen

A middle-European cake for Christmas and New Year

20 g (¾ oz) fresh yeast or
1 sachet dried yeast
¼ cup water, lukewarm for
fresh yeast, warm for dried
yeast
¾ cup milk, lukewarm for
fresh yeast, warm for dried
yeast
1 level teaspoon salt
¹/₃ cup sugar
²/₃ cup soft unsalted butter
2 eggs at room temperature,
lightly beaten
finely grated rind of 1 lemon
3½ to 4 cups bread making
flour or plain (all-purpose)
flour sifted with 2 level
teaspoons gluten flour
¼ cup sultanas (golden
raisins)
¼ cup chopped mixed
(candied) peel
¼ cup glacé (candied)
cherries, halved
¼ cup chopped almonds
extra melted butter
extra sugar

GLAZE AND DECORATION
beaten egg with a little water
icing (confectioners') sugar

BY HAND

PLACE THE YEAST in a large mixing bowl, add the water and stir until the yeast dissolves. Add the milk, salt, sugar, butter, eggs, lemon rind and half of the flour and beat very well with a wooden spoon. Add almost all of the remaining flour, a half a cupful at a time. When the dough becomes too stiff for the spoon, use just one floured hand to knead the dough in the bowl.

TURN THE DOUGH onto a lightly floured board and knead for five minutes or until the dough no longer sticks to your hands or the board and it is smooth and elastic. Use just a very light sprinkling of flour on the board to stop the dough from sticking.

BY MIXER

PLACE THE YEAST and water in a large mixer bowl. Stir to dissolve yeast. Add the milk, salt, sugar, butter, eggs, lemon rind and almost all of the flour and mix, using the dough hook and a low speed, until the dough comes together and leaves the sides and bottom of the bowl. Knead for three minutes, adding the extra flour if necessary. Knead by hand on a lightly floured board for one minute or until the dough is no longer sticky.

BY FOOD PROCESSOR

PLACE THE YEAST and water in the food processor bowl fitted with the steel blade. Pulse for 10 seconds to mix. Add the milk, salt, sugar, butter, eggs, lemon rind and almost all of the flour and process, with several pulses to mix, for about one minute. Add enough of the remaining flour so that the dough comes together. Knead by hand on a lightly floured board for one minute or until the dough is no longer sticky.

If you have a small food processor, process the dough in two batches and do not overwork dough.

THE NEXT STEP

PLACE THE DOUGH in a lightly oiled bowl and turn dough over so that it is very thinly coated all over with oil. Put the bowl in a large plastic bag and leave in a warm place until the dough has doubled in size.

PUNCH DOWN and knead for 10 seconds so that the dough is back to its original size.

KNEAD IN the peel, fruit and almonds. Divide the dough in half and roll one half into an oval about 25 x 18 cm (10 x 7 in). Brush with extra melted butter and sprinkle with the extra sugar. Fold over lengthwise, not quite in half, so the edges are within 1 cm (½ in) of meeting. Place on a greased baking tray and cover with a dry cloth. Repeat with the second half of the dough. Leave to rise until doubled in size again. Brush with beaten egg glaze.

PREHEAT OVEN to moderate (180°C/350°F).

BAKE FOR 35 to 40 minutes or until the loaves sounds hollow when tapped on the bottom and there is no stale beer smell. Cool on a wire rack. When cold, dust thickly with icing sugar.

TO MAKE a marzipan stollen, soften prepared marzipan with a little egg white and shape into a log and place in the centre of the dough before folding in half.

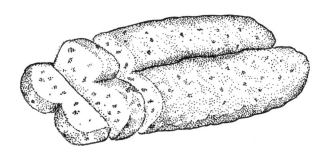

Facts and Information

Questions and Answers

If you are happy with the way your bread tastes and looks, and if everyone is eating up every last crumb, don't bother to read this — you don't need it. If, however, you are a perfectionist or you aren't pleased with your results and people aren't eating your bread, even if it is just out of the oven with lots of butter and honey, and the birds are leaving it too, read on. You may find a solution here. There are also answers to those questions most asked in bread making classes.

Q.
Why are my loaves so tiny?
A.
You may have not let it rise enough or you may have used too much salt. If your oven was too hot there may not have been enough time for a final rise before the yeast was killed.

Q.
What has caused my loaves to sink during baking?
A.
The loaves have been allowed to over-rise in their pans before baking. Next time this happens, punch down and re-shape. Allow to rise again, then bake.

Q.
Why does my bread have such a coarse texture?
A.
It could be that the rising time was too long, or the oven was too cool, or the bread wasn't kneaded enough or you used too little flour.

Q.

Why is my bread so crumbly?

A.

Not enough kneading or too much flour or the oven was too cool. Breads made with only wholemeal flour are often crumbly.

Q.

Why does my bread have such a hard crust?

A.

It's possible your oven was not hot enough or the dough may have been risen in too hot a place or you cooked it for too long.

Q.

Why do my plaited breads always run together and lose their shape?

A.

It may be due to over-rising or rising in too warm a place. Next time, re-shape them and let them rise in a cooler spot.

Q.

What do I do when my dough has over-risen in the pans?

A.

Punch down, re-knead and re-shape and allow to rise again.

Q.

Why is my bread so pale looking?

A.

You may have used too little salt or the oven may not have been hot enough.

Q.

Why do most bread recipes allow for such a variation in the amount of flour used?

A.

The amount of flour that can be kneaded into dough varies because of the humidity, the temperature of the room, the temperature of the flour and the moisture content of the flour.

Q.

How can I tell when enough flour is added when I am kneading?

A.

If the dough no longer sticks to your hands or the surface of the board, you've kneaded in enough flour. Wholemeal and rye doughs are always sticky if you poke your fingers into them so be careful not to work in too much flour.

Q.

Is it possible to knead too much?

A.

Yes, but this usually only happens when an electric mixer with a dough hook is doing the work. Only knead for a maximum of five minutes if you are using one.

Q.

Do I need a special recipe for rolls?

A.

No, most bread recipes can be used for rolls.

Q.

Why isn't my wholemeal bread rising?

A.

Wholemeal and rye breads can take longer to rise than white doughs. Just give them more time.

Q.

How long does it take for the dough to rise the first time?

A.

This will vary from dough to dough but for a dough with 20 g ($^{3}/_{4}$ oz) yeast or 1 sachet of dried yeast and four cups of white flour, and in an environment of 26°C/80°F, it may take between 45 minutes to an hour.

Q.

How long does it take for the dough to rise the second time?

A.

It usually takes half the time of the first rising.

Q.

My breads taste great but why are they uneven and lumpy?

A.

If you take greater care with shaping, don't put too much dough in the pans and allow a longer rising time you should get a better shaped loaf.

A Glossary of Flours and Bread Stuffs

ALL-PURPOSE FLOUR

The American name for plain flour.

BARLEY FLOUR

This flour contains no gluten and needs to be mixed with wheat flour, either white bread making flour or wholemeal (whole-wheat) flour. It makes a moist, sweet, fine textured bread and can be lightly roasted for a different flavour.

BRAN

Bran is the outer covering of the wheat kernel, oat or rice grain and is ground with the whole grain or removed and ground separately. It gives the bread a good texture and also provides roughage.

BREAD IMPROVERS

Commercial bakers add bread improvers, such as malted flour, to doughs to remove the need for a second rising of doughs. Double risen doughs, like most of the recipes in this book, rise more slowly and have much more flavour and character.

BREAD MAKING FLOUR

This is flour made from 'hard' wheat. It has the right amount of the protein gluten to produce quality bread with fine texture. It is not generally available in supermarkets, although some plain flours sold there are high in gluten, but it can be found in health food shops in small quantities or bought directly from a commercial flour mill.

BREAKFAST CEREALS

Many breakfast cereals can be added to bread doughs. Try corn or bran flakes, muesli, bran cereal, shredded wheat or rice bubbles. If you are using a sugary cereal cut down or delete the sugar in the recipe.

BUCKWHEAT FLOUR

Buckwheat has no gluten and should be mixed with wheat flour, either white bread making flour or wholemeal (whole-wheat) flour. The flour is dark with a distinctive flavour and is used in pumpernickel and black breads.

CORNMEAL (POLENTA)

Cornmeal is available in either yellow or white. Since it lacks gluten, it makes a very heavy loaf by itself and is best when mixed with wheat flour. A little cornmeal in white bread gives an interesting texture. When sprinkled onto baking trays it gives the bread a crunchy base.

GLUTEN FLOUR

This is made from the protein substance in the whole grain of the wheat and it gives elasticity to dough. It becomes sticky when mixed with water and may be blown up with air, or any other gas, and it sets when baked. It can be added to any flour to increase the gluten content but it must be sifted and dispersed through the flour otherwise it will form into solid lumps.

LECITHIN GRANULES

Lecithin granules have the same emulsifying effect as eggs. Use 2 level teaspoons of granules as a substitute for each egg.

MILLET FLOUR

This flour makes a nutritious and tasty bread when mixed with wheat flour, either white bread making flour or wholemeal (wholewheat) flour. In a loaf with four cups of flour, substitute up to two cups of millet flour.

PLAIN FLOUR (ALL-PURPOSE)

This is generally a blend of 'hard' and 'soft' wheats. Hard wheat is high in the protein gluten and is used for bread. Soft wheats are lower in protein and make better biscuits, cakes and pastries. Plain (all-purpose) flour can be used in bread making if one teaspoon of gluten flour is sifted with each cup of flour.

OAT FLOUR

This is finely ground flour from the whole-oat kernel and needs to be mixed with wheat flour. It can easily be made at home by blending porridge-style rolled oats finely in your blender. A food processor will make a coarser grind which can also be used.

OATMEAL (ROLLED OATS)

Oatmeal may be used either cooked or uncooked and makes a very moist sweet bread. As it contains no gluten, it must be mixed with wheat flour. Old fashioned rolled oats have a better flavour than the instant ones but either can be used.

POTATO FLOUR

Potato flour must be blended with wheat flour and it makes a moist, dense, long lasting loaf.

RICE FLOUR

Rice flour is ground from broken grains and it can replace up to 30% of wheat flour in a bread recipe. Breads with rice flour are dark, heavy and sweet.

RYE FLOUR

Rye is the only flour besides wheat to contain gluten. However, the gluten content is lower and it needs the addition of some wheat flour, either white bread making flour or wholemeal (whole-wheat) flour, if you want to have a high light loaf. All rye doughs are difficult to handle but the bread is fine textured and moist.

SOY FLOUR

Soy flour is lacking in gluten and needs to be mixed with wheat flour, either white bread making flour or wholemeal (whole-wheat) flour. As it has a strong distinctive taste, use it sparingly. You can omit the second rising with doughs made with soy flour. Shape after kneading, let rise until doubled and then bake.

WHOLEMEAL FLOUR (WHOLE-WHEAT)

This flour contains all of the wheat kernel including the bran and the germ. When it is used on its own, it makes a heavy flat bread. For a lighter loaf, mix it with white bread making flour.

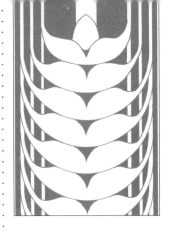

Weights, Measures and Oven Temperatures

These recipes were tested using Australian standard metric measures of 250 ml (millilitre) measuring cups, 20 ml tablespoons, 5 ml teaspoons and half and quarter teaspoons. There is a slight variation in other countries' cup and teaspoon measurements but none of the recipes in this book will be adversely affected if non-Australian measuring cups and spoons are used.

Just be sure you use the same cup measure for everything — the flour, the water, the other liquids — otherwise you may end up with dough which is too stiff and is very difficult, if not impossible, to put right. A dough which is too soft is easy — it just needs more flour.

Country	Cup	Tablespoon	Teaspoon
America	237 ml	14.8 ml	4.9 ml
Canada	227 ml	14.2 ml	4.74 ml
New Zealand	250 ml	15 ml	5 ml
United Kingdom	300 ml	17.7 ml	5 ml
Australia	250 ml	20 ml	5 ml

Oven Information

Always preheat the oven. When baking in a pan, place the pans in the centre of the lowest shelf with at least 5 cm (2 in) of space between them. Free-form breads on baking trays are best baked in the centre of the oven, one at a time. In the first 10 minutes of baking the heat of the oven gives the final boost of rising to the yeast before it dies and, after this time, you can open and close the oven without it affecting the shape of the bread.

Use these temperatures as a rough guide only as ovens vary. If you are using a fan forced electric oven, read the manual and follow the manufacturer's instructions or, if you have lost the instructions, reduce temperatures by 20°C/68°F and reduce the cooking time.

	°C	°F	★Gas Mark
Very cool	110	225	1/2 or 1
Cool	140	275	2 or 4
Moderately slow	160	325	3 or 4
Moderate	180	350	5 or 7
Moderately hot	200	400	7 or 9
Hot	220	425	8 or 10
Very hot	250	475	9 or 12

★Choose the setting that is right for your gas oven.

Index